Black Paper Basics

Ten Points

1 Children are not naturally good. They need firm, tactful discipline from parents and teachers with clear standards. Too much freedom for children breeds selfishness, vandalism and personal unhappiness.

2 If the non-competitive ethos of progressive education is allowed to dominate our schools, we shall produce a generation unable to maintain our standards of living when opposed by fierce rivalry from overseas competitors.

3 It is the quality of teachers which matters, rather than their numbers or their equipment. We have sacrificed quality for numbers, and the result has been a lowering of standards. We need high-quality, higher-paid teachers in the classroom, not as counsellors or administrators.

4 Schools are for schooling, not social engineering.

5 The best way to help children in deprived areas is to teach them to be literate and numerate, and to develop all their potential abilities.

6 Every normal child should be able to read by the age of seven. This can be achieved by the hard work of teachers who use a structured approach.

7 Without selection the clever working-class child in a deprived area stands little chance of a real academic education.

8 External examinations are essential for schools, colleges, polytechnics and universities. Without such checks, standards decline. Working-class children suffer when applying for jobs if they cannot bring forward proof of their worth achieved in authoritative examinations.

9 Freedom of speech must be preserved in universities. Institutions which cannot maintain proper standards of open debate should be closed.

10 You can have equality or equality of opportunity; you cannot have both. Equality will mean the holding back (or the new deprivation) of the brighter children.

Contents

Letter to MPs and Parents

C. B. COX and RHODES BOYSON

I

In the late 1960s it seemed that the educational revolution in the United Kingdom would wreak its havoc with little or no opposition. The retreat from teaching and structure, the flight from high culture to pop culture, the move to non-selective education, still advanced on all sides and even influenced the programmes of political parties. These phenomena were, moreover, by no means confined to this country, but raised questions which are internationally important, particularly in America.

The original *Black Paper*, published in February 1969, was the first serious attempt in Britain to provide a critique of the move to progressive education; the howls of rage which met its appearance rivalled those which arise in some theocracy if the predominant faith is challenged. This *Black Paper* pointed out the message that the whole educational revolution was proceeding on the basis of justification by faith and not by works. Even the Plowden Report—which represented the height of progressive euphoria—was based on figures of advances in reading standards which were really invalid.

Black Papers Two and *Three* strengthened the critique of progressive and non-selective and egalitarian education. At last the tens of thousands of teachers who secretly opposed its advance realized that their opposition was firmly based; whatever faults there were in the preceding traditional system were as nothing compared with the strange excesses of destructive zeal by the progressives (or, as we prefer to call them, the 'experimentalists', who are usually working with other people's children).

II

Five years have elapsed since *Black Paper Three* and it is again time to survey the educational scene. Expenditure has further increased, the pupil-teacher ratio has fallen, teacher training has lengthened, the school-leaving age has been raised, there are more in higher education; but it is doubtful if there has been any advance in real terms.

Start and Wells and T. R. Horton's surveys of reading standards of 11 and 15 year olds indicate that literacy is declining. Half the adult illiterates are below the age of 25. Industry complains of increasing innumeracy. Some 650,000 children play truant every day from our schools and teachers flee from city schools because of lesson-resistance and insolence by the pupils. Adolescent violence increases and universities show signs of a student and staff intolerance of free discussion which threatens a new dark age. Genuine cultural participation falls steadily and a non-value pop culture becomes dominant.

Parents complain of their children not being taught in primary schools; they make major sacrifices to remove their children from secondary schools where indiscipline is rife and scholarship non-existent. Hypocrisy is common-place; our educational rulers and administrators have their children educated in ways they would prohibit for other people's children. The educational scene is very sick indeed.

It was once alleged that what was good for General Motors was good for America. The educational establishment, which is largely a self-seeking industry, now holds that what is good for education is good for Britain (or America). Ivan Illich is right when he points to the dangers of an educational priesthood largely serving its own interests.

The problem is not one of money. It is no good a church demanding more sacrifices from its congregation when it doesn't offer hopes of true salvation. It is no good education clamouring for more money when every additional pound seems to increase the problems, lower standards and increase the widespread cynicism.

III

It is time, however, that we in the *Black Papers* not only criticized but suggested what should be done. Let us look at each section of education and make positive suggestions which the educational administration and the politicians could apply. We shall also increase the strength of the National Council for Educational Standards by regular bulletins and meetings, so that we shall channel the great interest of parents to demand reform if all else fails.

Nursery schools may be of great use in deprived city centres; but all the evidence from America points to the fact that children advance most quickly where attempts are made to strengthen the mother's direct involvement in the learning experiences of her offspring. The family is the primary unit of society and the cycle of deprivation will not be broken by removing children from it except in extreme cases. Income tax should be remodelled so that it advantages mothers with children below the age of 5 to stay at home and look after them instead of going to work.

Infant and junior schools should again be teaching units with syllabuses and specific standards of attainment for varied groups of children. All children without brain damage should be reading at the age of 7. There should be national examinations to enforce this. The fact that the National Children's Bureau found that 37% of children needed help in the junior school (7–11) normally given in the infant school and that a further 10% had not begun to read is a national disgrace. Inability to read arises from bad

3

teaching or bad classroom discipline *not* from deprived home backgrounds.

Teachers should be teachers again and not social workers. Deprived children are not deprived unless they feel deprived; school should be the one place where they are treated as normal children and not social curiosities. Poor home conditions, parental neglect and even malnutrition and ill-treatment have always existed, but the traditional teacher by treating the pupils as pupils has opened the eyes of children to a new world of exciting and liberating learning. The teacher who uses poor social conditions as an excuse for poor teaching is the cause of greater deprivation than the home background itself. At a time of rising living standards since World War II the teacher by becoming a second-grade social worker has become a third-grade teacher. It is far easier to blame the lack of an internal water closet for the failure of a pupil to read than to slog at teaching that pupil to read.

We believe, unlike Christopher Jencks and others, that schools are very influential in teaching. In our experience one school in a deprived area will have 98% of its pupils reading up to their mental age at 11 while another will have a whole school reading below their mental age with some 40% virtual non-readers. Let the Colleges of Education concentrate again on training teachers, not on giving a third-class 'collage' education which doesn't fit their products for the classroom.

Teachers do not need longer training: all this has done is to persuade many able youngsters to enter some other profession. They want both a spell as a pupil-teacher apprentice to a skilled teacher and to be taught the techniques of teaching and a body of subject knowledge which they can pass on to their pupils. Nor do good honours degree graduates teaching sixth formers need a year's course which is nothing but the sort of restrictive practice which would be condemned in industry. Again this year's course deters many able graduates from trying teaching.

Reducing the pupil-teacher ratio has brought little or no advantage. There are numerous pieces of research pointing to the fact that, given a reasonable maximum, the size of class is unimportant but the calibre of teacher is all-important. The lowering of the pupil-teacher ratio has simply allowed the best teachers to leave the classroom for counselling and administration and the calibre of the classroom teacher has fallen. Indeed the status of the classroom teacher is reduced by the fact that only apparent failures remain there. If every deputy head, counsellor, year master and housemaster in the large London comprehensive schools returned to teaching, there would not only be no teacher shortage but there would be far fewer disciplinary problems because the most capable teachers were teaching again. Special allowances should be paid for extra work performed outside school time.

The classroom teacher whose results were outstanding could be paid an extra £500 or £1,000 a year to train for a year an apprentice teacher. This would do a great deal both for the status of the teacher and the training of new teachers. Lecturers in education in Colleges and Departments of Education should have to spend five years back in the classroom for every five years of lecturing, and no student should ever hear a lecturer lecture until he has seen him teach in a classroom.

Both the major political parties have moved towards the establishment of national standards. These could be laid down for the 7, 11 and 14 year old and should be *minimum* standards for all pupils of over 70 I.Q. There was once an understood curriculum throughout the whole country but this disappeared some ten years ago when the liberation of the pupil and the development of interests and projects waxed supreme. This has meant that a boy or girl is

dependent for his education or non-education on the lottery of the state school system. One primary school will have good teaching and a tight syllabus of work to be covered and the pupils will leave well educated; another school will have imaginative teaching but little syllabus control and pupils will leave with pockets of knowledge and pockets of ignorance, while a third school will have poor teaching and no syllabus structure and pupils will leave ignorant and deprived.

The 7+ examination should cover literacy and numeracy and pupils should be expected to pass such a test before they proceeded to junior school. The 11+ and 14+ tests should also cover a body of minimum geographical, historical, scientific and literary knowledge. Teachers could teach beyond these basic syllabuses and could introduce other subjects; but such syllabuses would ensure that all schools offered a reasonable education, which is not now the case. Teacher and school liberty has become licence, to the deprivation of pupils who suffer from the whims and prejudices of teachers.

It will be a pity if at a time when the progressive shibboleths of reading readiness, free expression, team teaching, and integrated days are in retreat if the cheapness of building open-plan schools means that such schools, which predetermine such teaching, continue to be built. Knowing how desperately teachers struggled to get away from the nineteenth-century open-plan schools to individual classrooms it will be a tragedy if an alliance of progressive educationalists and county treasurers brings back such outdated school buildings.

IV

Over the last five years there have been changes in the debate on secondary schools. The Labour Party is unfortunately still committed to the comprehensive neighbourhood non-selective school despite its growing unpopularity and increasing evidence of its academic ineffectiveness, with children of all ability levels. The Liberal Party tags behind the Labour Party on this issue. The Conservative Party, realizing the disillusionment of its grass-roots support, has moved to partial opposition in so far as it would now defend existing selective schools and would even encourage the building of new selective schools.

It is very likely that the evidence of declining academic standards in comprehensive schools could bring, as in America, the creation of single-subject specialist schools in mathematics, science, languages and other subjects. There is a similar development in Russia and Eastern Europe. Certainly the pattern of schools will diversify again.

There are a variety of means whereby schools can again be made responsive to the wishes of parents. The Conservative Party has suggested the election of more parent governors. The introduction of the educational voucher (see p. 27) in two trial areas in this country, which would really give parents control of schools, would be widely welcomed. Real parental choice is offered in Denmark where if 85 parents wish to open their own school they gain full support from public funds. Belgium and the Netherlands have somewhat similar schemes. Such a scheme could be tried in Britain and real radical experiments would be possible while the enforcement of the 7+, 11+ and 14+ national tests, and of course the 'O' level and 'A' level G.C.E. examinations, would guarantee standards.

We defend the right of parents to make sacrifices for the better or more varied education of their children, but the vast majority of our children attend state schools and these must be made to work. The fact that approaching 50% of our secondary pupils now attend comprehensive schools also brings the corollary that these must be made to work. The 14+ test, which could also be a school leaving examination, would help. The disappearance to apprenticeships and work of the 14 + lesson-resisters would also be of considerable help. The enforcement of school attendance on such pupils brings major classroom disturbances, while the non-enforcement of attendance creates a sub-criminal class living on the fringe of society, worthy of the pen of Dickens.

The American voucher experiment at San José, California, points to a possible improvement which could transform the comprehensive schools. Each school in San José offers a variety of courses and parents choose within as well as between schools. Most schools there have four distinct courses: the mathematics-science programme which is very academically demanding, the easier fine arts course, the 'three Rs plus' programme and the creative arts industrial training for the less academically gifted. Pupils and parents choose their own course.

With rising dissatisfaction about many comprehensive schools it could be that the time is ripe to demand (and if necessary legislate for) the introduction of at least four distinct courses in each large comprehensive school while small comprehensive schools offered one or two courses. It is, with rare exceptions, the non-streamed common or no-curriculum comprehensive school which creates most resentment, has the lowest academic standards and the greatest problems with truancy and violence. Comprehensive schools with strict and separate mini-school courses were what many of us first supported when we came out in favour of the comprehensive school and it is perhaps time we returned to this form of organization.

V

Higher education, like school education, clamours for more money. Here again instead of huge increases in financial aid there needs to be a rethinking of fundamental purposes. During the last ten years universities have declined rapidly in reputation because of the disruptive activities of some students, and the failure of staff to maintain standards of discipline and free speech. Sit-ins and violence have made students unpopular with the general public, and one result has been little sympathy for demands for increased grants.

It has recently become clear that there is no longer any need for major expansion in institutions of higher education. In both universities and polytechnics there are vacant places in the sciences, engineering and technology. During the last two years universities have been lowering standards, even in the Arts and Social Sciences, to achieve their entry targets (details of the shortfall are given in the article on 'Educational Statistics' (pp. 36–39). There are exceptions, particularly medicine and law, for which the demand is still great. But the needs of such subjects may be partly met by redeployment of resources from subjects which no longer attract sufficient students. The Utopian visions of the post-Robbins era have been proved unrealizable.

It is to be hoped that we shall grasp the opportunities presented by this new situation. Instead of diluting standards, we should try to maintain traditions of excellence, and to improve teaching and research. The idea of the comprehensive university must be rejected. Those who support open entry for young people without proper qualifications must be made aware of the amount of human suffering such projects engender. The 'open admissions' system in New York allows access to universities to thousands of unacademic young people, who spend much of their time in listless boredom in coffee bars. Many become drop-outs. In the mid-1960s there was a general feeling that all children and students would enjoy and profit from extra years of study. We now know that a large percentage of young people, including many who are highly intelligent, do not want to spend early adulthood in institutions of learning. We should not despise them for

this. We should not produce a society which suggests to such youngsters that there is something wrong with them if they do not wish to stay at school or go to university. We should recognize their right to choose for themselves. The articles we print here about universities in the United States depict the harm done when large numbers of young people, many without the desire to study, are forced by social pressures into universities.

VI

In higher education there must be no national plan. We need a plurality of institutions offering a wide variety of choice to students of different abilities and aims. Institutions that fail, that cannot attract students, or cannot maintain standards of open debate, should be closed. Transfer from one kind of institution to another, from college of education to university, for example, should be possible for good students.

Many students lack a reasonable background of general education. There should be a new matriculation requirement that university entrants should have at least seven 'O' levels, including English language, maths, a science and a foreign language. Non-university entrants, of course, could continue to take single subjects at 'O' level as they do now.

At present British undergraduates study for no more than about thirty weeks a year. The majority spend the rest of their time working for money in a variety of jobs, and do very little study in vacations. This situation is ridiculous. Three terms of twelve weeks each would be a sensible arrangement. The extra teaching demands on staff should be balanced by increases in sabbatical leave, particularly for successful researchers.

Most university teachers are appointed in their mid-twenties, and can be almost certain of tenure for life. They are on probation for three or four years, but it is rare for anyone to be sacked. With the small number of senior appointments available, many can expect to stay in the same institution until they retire. This breeds stagnation. We advocate that junior academics should be placed on five-year contracts, and there should be no tenure until after at least ten years in the profession. It would be usual to change institutions after five years, and colleges, polytechnics and universities would advertise vacancies specifically for those who had completed five-year contracts elsewhere. This would create flexibility and liveliness, and encourage able young staff to work hard for promotion.

VII

The progressive bandwagon still rolls on, but in the current slowing-down phase we receive hundreds of letters and reports from teachers about the confusion in schools, the damage being inflicted on young lives. Our correspondents usually ask to be kept anonymous, because if they publicly opposed the known views of local inspectors and education officers their promotion prospects would be blighted. We print two typical examples from class teachers on pages 30 and 31.

Our contributors include supporters of different political parties; they are at one in their belief in free speech and high standards in education. Iris Murdoch writes in the opening article:

Why should socialist policy, of all things, be so grossly unjust to the underprivileged clever child, avid to learn, able to learn, and under non-selective education likely to pass in relaxed idle boredom those precious years when strenuous learning is a joy and when the whole intellectual and moral future of the human being is at stake? (p. 9)

G. Kenneth Green has wide experience of comprehensive

schools. He was headmaster of Swinton Comprehensive School, West Riding, where he amalgamated two schools, a secondary modern and a secondary technical; then head of Thomas Calton School, S.E.15, which was in two main buildings and two subsidiary buildings all on different sites; then head of Pimlico School, S.W.1, where he amalgamated four schools, a boys' and girls' grammar school, a boys' technical school and a co-educational secondary modern. His criticism of comprehensive education reflects the views of large numbers of teachers who have participated in recent experiments. Fred Naylor, who contributes an article on comprehensives, was head of Bath Technical School in the 1960s, and then for five years Sixth Form Curriculum and Examinations Officer at the Schools Council. He describes American and Russian experiments in comprehensive education, still largely unknown and ignored in the United Kingdom. Our contributions from America underline how similar are educational problems in the States, and how we should learn from their mistakes.

G. H. Bantock's article is a detailed analysis of progressive ideas and their influence on school curricula. He argues that progressive educationists are committed to two contradictory sets of values. They believe in the importance of the individual, and this should persuade them to allow able children to advance as fast as possible. They also believe in equality, and this leads to collectivism, uniformity, instinctive faith in non-streaming. The lack of clear educational goals is a major cause of the failure of comprehensive education. Bernice Martin examines the sociological and intellectual background of educational permissiveness, and points out the dangerous irrationality of modern fashions. The lack of structure in progressive education particularly harms working-class children.

Stuart Froome, member of the Bullock Committee, joins with George Weber, Deputy Director of the American Council for Basic Education, in demanding a return to formal teaching of reading based on phonic methods. Dr Jeanne Chall's *Learning to Read: The Great Debate*, a summary of all relevant research, changed the course of reading instruction in the United States, yet its conclusions are still not sufficiently well known in Britain.

Max Beloff defines the conditions in which academic freedoms and standards of excellence survive. He writes:

> Instead of apologizing for their own existence and privileges and attempting to meet their critics half-way, they [universities] need leaders who will be absolutely intransigent about fundamentals whether the challenge comes from politicians, from their own students, or from the traitors in their midst. (p. 49)

These words can be applied to all branches of education. *Black Paper 1975* is a call to all politicians, parents and teachers to be absolutely intransigent about fundamentals.

We end with an appeal to parents. Attend parents' meetings. Apply pressure on your local school to maintain standards. Do not be put off by progressive excuses about low standards of reading, writing, spelling and arithmetic. Demand higher standards of behaviour in school. This *Black Paper* gives you information and arguments to help you oppose dangerous fashions which have corrupted many in the teaching profession. If you fail, your children will join the new class of the deprived, those denied the great benefits of traditional schooling.

Socialism
and Selection

IRIS MURDOCH

Fortunately we live in a tolerant country where, on the whole, controversial issues can still be discussed calmly, without rage, even with humour. Of course education is a subject which arouses strong feelings and where serious well-intentioned people differ. The existing educational system is complex and deeply rooted and incarnates values which are of slow growth and dear to many. It seems to me that what is needed is careful piecemeal compromise, rather than quick destruction and radical experiment. In any case, let us try to discuss it quietly, use clear ordinary language, not obscure jargon or brutal rhetoric, and keep in mind that while theories are fighting individual children are growing up.

I am not an opponent of comprehensive schools as such, unless they are by definition non-selective. These schools are frequently too big and have the inevitable disadvantage of being new and experimental. No doubt the idea of the comprehensive school, and the schools themselves, will change and improve in time. I certainly think it tragic that the cause of comprehensive schooling, which is still a controversial one, should be taken by many of our leaders to involve the rapid destruction of other types of school. Our democracy has always drawn its strength from various centres of power, and this has been one of its characteristic virtues. Schools are like states, easier to destroy than to build, and with merits which are not readily transplanted. A good school is a remarkable and highly individual creation. The comprehensive experiment is only beginning. Why should not the different systems coexist in a mixed educational economy and help and inform each other? Many grammar schools and independent schools are very good indeed. The fact that not all parents have access to them is not in itself a reason for closing these schools, unless envy counts as a reason. The fates of individual children are at stake and parents are rightly unwilling to deprive their children of a good education simply because others are less fortunate. It does not seem to me that the state should interfere to remove these blessings. Rather the state should, through an extension of the direct grant system, attempt to distribute them more widely. This could, with an inconsistency and ability to compromise which is characteristic of British arrangements, be perfectly compatible with the forwarding of the comprehensive experiment.

Why is this not a socialist programme for education, as I personally, as a socialist, think that it ought to be? Why does even the suggestion of such a programme make many people on the left so angry? I suspect that perhaps the main reason is that a deep primary judgment has been made against the idea of selection in education; and those who already object to grammar schools as being selective and separatist are not likely to interest themselves in the technicalities of how to 'democratize' the even more separatist independent schools, especially as the most obvious method would be by selection on merit. The prior judgment against selection thereby effectively closes the whole discussion.

The arguments for and against selection depend partly upon factual disagreements and partly upon radical differences of value, and it is no doubt the latter that occasion the anger on both sides. Of course the factual considerations become evaluative through the amount of 'weight' and 'colour' which is given to them, but it is possible at least to begin such a discussion by marshalling facts. The objections to a selective system might be said to be these. Selection must depend upon a method of assessment, examinations or a substitute, and this causes an anxiety to children, which may in some cases actually interfere with their ability to learn. Those who fail academically are given an unreasonable sense of inferiority, and if separated from clever pupils may feel even more inferior. The presence of the clever, on the other hand, can help and inspire the less clever. Further, in areas where the more educationally advanced children tend to be middle class, a non-selective mixing will promote social equality. I think the last of these arguments is often felt to be the strongest.

The factual aspects of the matter can of course plausibly be stated the other way round. The presence of clever children makes the others feel inferior, the less clever are just as likely to retard the clever as the latter are to inspire the former, a mixed class is likely to contain a group of thoroughly bored children, mixed-ability teaching works best with small classes of docile pupils with roughly similar backgrounds, but demands very exceptional teachers when these conditions are not satisfied. To be concerned about the fate of the clever child is not to be indifferent to the fate of the less clever. The latter, just as much as the former, needs specialized teaching and it is unreasonable to expect teachers to be universal geniuses who can teach every sort of child. 'Streaming', in the sense of selective attention, must occur somewhere, and is it not better to do this on some general rational basis, rather than leaving it to the unfortunate teacher to 'stream' the class, which will often mean in practice placating the noisiest group? As for examinations, they need not be the only method of selection (though I personally think they are the best); and the removal of anxiety may be less important

7

than the loss of a more exacting education. If selection is in general desirable then its uncomfortable concomitants must be put up with, and the disadvantages seem to me to be open to intelligent amelioration, and in any case to carry much less weight than the advantages.

The argument about 'social mixing' is a powerful one. Everyone should 'muck in together', children of all kinds should be friends and should be aware of how others live. Well-off parents and poor parents should be together at parents' meetings. Such mixing can only be a social benefit. I think I agree, and if this is the fundamental idea in the argument I feel sympathy with it. However, this is not an objection to selection as such, since social mixing takes place in a streamed comprehensive school. Further, and assuming a case where non-selection favours mixing, the mixing may be less important than the more vigorous teaching which clever children receive as a result of selection. How one assesses this, and other, arguments against selection will depend on whether it is felt that clever children benefit academically from selection, and how valuable such a 'benefit' is considered to be.

That it is easier to teach a difficult subject, for instance advanced mathematics or the advanced stages of a language, to a group of selected, academically clever children than to a mixed-ability group is surely a fact. Those who object to the existence of such 'hard-learning groups' may of course do so because they think that other things are more important than learning. Theories of 'spontaneous schooling', for instance (let the children learn what they want when they want it), usually admit to having in view advantages that are not purely academic: absence of anxiety, a more balanced 'all-round' interest in the world and so on. It would certainly be naïve to think that most of the children who were capable of doing so would spontaneously want to learn Russian or algebra. It would also be naïve to imagine that early schooling does not matter because 'it can all be done later' as an adult. Adult learning is in obvious ways a different and often more difficult enterprise. Childhood is learning time. (Compare one's knowledge of a language learnt at school with one's knowledge of a language learnt as an adult.) The aim of becoming an all-round human being is certainly a worthy one, but a clever person should become an all-round *clever* person; and few things are more agonizing and anxious-making, both in childhood and later, than to feel that one has not had the academic advantages which one deserved. Such agony was felt by many of the original leaders of the labour and trade union movement, who fought hard for just selective education: it is indeed bizarre to see their successors treating academic schooling as an enemy.

It often seems when such matters are being discussed that selection is opposed because it involves a recognition of intellectual excellence, and of some people being in this respect better than others. Under the régime of non-selection there would be no (a phrase in use here) 'sheep and goats'. The arguments above for not recognizing the existence of sheep and goats (arguments concerned with 'inferiority', 'anxiety', etc.) seem to me to be flimsy compared with the importance of acknowledging that there *are* sheep and goats, and acting accordingly. It is curious that it is only intellectual merit which is threatened with this unjust treatment. No-one speaks up for non-selective football. It is not thought in other fields that there is anything objectionable either in selecting and training promising youngsters, or in admiring and revering those who ultimately excel. And this is surely right. Admiration of excellence is proper and comely. When we admire a great singer or footballer or actor or violinist we do not feel that we are doing something shameful and demeaning to ourselves. We are not made miserable and envious when we

delight in talents which we have not got; we are grateful because our world has been enlarged and enriched by a vision of excellence which we can appreciate. This is the proper place of excellence in human life, as an inspiration to those who can compete and a pure delight to the others. (The only exception to this formulation is morality where of course everyone must compete. Moral excellence is not a spectator sport.) Why should intellectual merit alone be denied fostering and respect? Is not this thoroughly unjust to clever people and also dangerous to society? There seems little likelihood that intellectual superiority will 'out-glamourize' other kinds of skill among the young, thereby causing the unclever to despair. What seems a greater danger is a tendency to undervalue intellect and academic attainment, to despise the 'brainy', to resent the bookish, and thereby to encourage the dangerous and ever-present tendency of the inarticulate to hate the articulate. One has seen the results in other (so far) less happy lands of a general movement against 'the intellectuals'.

Even without frightening ourselves with such prospects we should be sufficiently alarmed at the lowering of academic standards which seems to be envisaged and accepted by those who advocate non-selective schooling and even speak calmly of non-selective universities. We are not, it seems to me, being simply asked to choose, as a temporary expedient while our educational system is academically improved, between a middling standard for all and a high standard for a few together with a lower standard for the rest. If an academic education for many more children were the aim, then one could set about rationally arguing that the universal application of non-streamed comprehensive schooling was not the way to achieve it. It seems rather that the idea of 'the academic' as something to which all should have, on merit, free access is itself being rejected by the Labour Party. We are being asked to accept an educational method which will permanently militate against intellect and which, by lowering standards 'at the top', will remove even the vista of this kind of excellence from those who might appreciate it and be inspired by it. The absence of this 'top' academic world would not only deprive our community of trained experts and leaders, it would soften the fibre of the whole educational system: a system which even now contains children who cannot read at eleven. We need more, not less of the academic; and there is nothing wrong with competition as the honest attempt to do one's best at a hard subject.

Education means this. All children should be taught, in so far as they are able to take it in, to distinguish getting things right from getting things wrong, to *read* and to value reading, to write their own language correctly (thinking is grammar). Education is the inculcation of a sense of scale. The educated person can not only distinguish accuracy from muddle, he can see how great great thinkers and great artists are. First lesson at the university: that one is far below the great scholars: humility, reverence for greatness, a realization of the difficulty of serious study. A non-selective system makes the teaching of accuracy and truthfulness harder at all levels, and will do serious damage to our community if it begins to produce people who imagine that they are educated when they are not. Non-selective schooling will (already does) damage the universities because less preliminary training can be asked for. And we are even being told by some to tolerate the macabre vision of non-selective universities on the American state model (which many American educationalists now agree to be a mistake) where superficial self-indulgent messing around with a few books and a few ideas is mistaken for scholarship and science. We should not tolerate, much less encourage, ignorance and inaccuracy among those who are supposed to be trained; and if it appears that some of our leading citizens cannot speak or write correct English we should not accept this as a sign of 'democracy', but regard it as something to be corrected in the next generation. Of course those who tell us that 'there will be no selection at eleven or at sixteen or at any other age' cannot mean literally what they say, since scientists and technicians will have to be trained and will have to be selected for training upon their mathematical merit. It is other kinds of intellectual excellence, which can more easily be subjected to the non-selective régime, which will suffer more in the long run. Perhaps the tilting of the balance in favour of science and away from the humanities is actually the aim of some of those who oppose selection? If so it is a sinister aim.

Those who are upset by the educational programme of the left are sometimes told: don't worry, able children will get their education somehow all the same. This may be true of middle-class able children with moderately bookish homes and educationally ambitious parents behind them. Selection must and will take place in education and those who banish rational methods of selection are simply favouring irrational and accidental ones. The children who will be lost forever are the poor clever children with an illiterate background who on the 'chance' system are being denied the *right* to a strict academic education which can only be achieved on the basis of some sort of selection. Why should socialist policy, of all things, be so grossly unjust to the underprivileged clever child, avid to learn, able to learn, and under non-selective education likely to pass in relaxed idle boredom those precious years when strenuous learning is a joy and when the whole intellectual and moral future of the human being is at stake? It is most surprising that a Labour government should be indifferent to the fate of this very important group in our community. The denial of rigorous education to working-class children will in the long run militate against the very social mixing which is supposed to be the object of the exercise, if it turns out in the future that our only cultivated citizens are middle class. Not least of the dangers of such a situation is the possibility that learning itself may come to be regarded as a 'middle-class value', repugnant to those who hold 'proletarian values'. It would be hard to exaggerate the brutalizing effect of such a development.

Reading and the School Handicap Score

STUART FROOME

It is interesting for observers of the educational scene to note that as methods in British schools have become increasingly informal and a noticeable decline in standards of reading and writing has become associated with this trend, apologists for the new progressive modes of teaching seem to have become more and more concerned with such apparently irrelevant matters as the social background of the pupils in the schools. It might have been thought that in this egalitarian age it would have been considered indelicate or even highly improper for anyone to be interested in what is now generally known as the socio-economic status of parents, but such is not the case.

Using the Registrar General's classification of 1960 based on occupations, the social class to which a child belongs is determined by the kind of employment in which the father is engaged. There are five specified classes: 1. Professional, 2. Managerial, 3. Non-manual and Skilled Manual, 4. Semi-skilled, 5. Unskilled. These classifications are sometimes used in connection with tests of attainment in reading carried out by local education authorities, and the scores of the children are related for statistical purposes to the kind of home in which they have been reared. We note, for instance, that in the I.L.E.A. Literacy Surveys of 1968 and 1971, the proportion of poor readers in the semi-skilled and unskilled groups increased from 17.9% at age eight and 25.9% at age eleven to 22.0% and 28.8% respectively over the period. Similarly, in the reading tests carried out in Aberdeen in 1962 and 1972 on 2,500 children of the eight and eleven age groups, it was discovered that among those in Social Class 1 and 2 the average standard had improved or had been maintained, whereas among those in Social Classes 4 and 5 the average score was seriously below that of the same groups ten years earlier. On a much larger scale, the National Child Development Study of 1972 based on the yearly development of 15,468 children born in the United Kingdom in March 1958, also used the conventional social class groupings in its findings. As well as providing the slightly shocking information that of 11,000 seven-year-olds tested in 1965, no less than 47% needed the help in reading usually given in the infant school of whom 10% were virtual non-readers, it was also revealed that of the children from Social Class 5, 48% were poor readers as compared with 8% in Social Class 1.

This preoccupation with pupils' private family matters reached absurd proportions in research carried out for the Plowden Committee, where it was shown that other social variables besides that of father's occupation had an effect upon a child's performance in tests of school attainment. These included father's education, mother's education, the number of books in the home and the number of children in the family. These four environmental influences, together with father's occupation, combined to form a weighted sum known as the School Handicap Score (S.H.S.), and this bizarre form of social background assessment is in fact also used in a number of other developed countries, where, as in Britain, it is clearly shown that there is a close connection between children's reading performance and the kind of home from which they draw their origin and support.

Now this piece of research will surprise no-one who is involved with teaching children. It would be strange if children from homes in the managerial and professional classes were not likely to be more intelligent and teachable than those from the homes of semi-skilled and unskilled parents. Their good start, coupled with superior housing, food, supply of books and other cultural facilities, must give them certain advantages throughout their school life. However, as the late Professor Sir Cyril Burt pointed out, there is no hard and fast rule about the effects of home and heredity: 'It is responsible quite as much for differences between members of the same family as for resemblances.' As he further noted, Benjamin Franklin's father was a soap-boiler and Michael Faraday's a blacksmith, while we could all quote cases of the children of distinguished academics who were veritable dunces at school.

We must therefore cast some doubt upon the value of the research which produced the somewhat trite information quoted above. We must also ask ourselves whether it will be of the slightest advantage to a teacher faced with a difficult remedial group of six non-readers in a secondary school, to be told that three are from Social Class 5, two from Class 4 and one is a bank manager's son. Will the lowly social status of the three from Class 5 induce the teacher to believe that they are already working to full capacity and therefore require no extra pressure, whereas the bank manager's son's low achievement, under the advantage of a superior home, may be attributed to laziness or lack of effort? Can knowledge of home background help the teacher to deal with pupils' reading deficiencies, or is there a real danger that records of adverse home circumstances will be used as excuses for poor progress and falling standards?

During the past decade, as complaints of declining attainment, truancy, bad behaviour and violence in schools have been given much publicity, it has become customary to attribute these failings to the effect of children living in inner-city areas where housing is poor, facilities are sparse and the neighbourhood is termed 'deprived'. Such areas are called Educational Priority Areas, and in the Plowden Committee Report on the Primary School it was recommended that: 'As a matter of national policy "positive discrimination" should favour schools in neighbourhoods where children are most severely handicapped by home conditions, and the programme should be phased to make schools in the deprived areas as good as the best in the country.'

Now, no-one could disagree with the principle of providing additional financial aid towards the provision of more and better-paid teachers, more spacious and better-equipped school buildings and improved facilities of all kinds in these areas of educational priority. However, before attributing all our schooling ills in such localities to social deprivation, it might be prudent to consider if there are other factors in some of the schools themselves which have contributed to increased juvenile delinquency, truancy and declining standards of scholastic achievement. I believe there are.

As a case in point, not long ago I visited a very large I.L.E.A. comprehensive school in an educational priority area. It was indeed a very grim neighbourhood but the buildings were modern and the educational facilities excellent, while the teacher/pupil ratio was exceptionally good, in the region of one to 14.5 which is better than in most public schools. There was a high proportion of children from immigrant families and there was obviously much deprivation generally in the district. One could only feel great sympathy for the headmaster and his staff working in such a school, where we were told, that on entry at age eleven plus no less than 50% of the children had reading ages below nine.

In one of the classes, however, it was surprising to see the pupils sitting with their coats on, although in this well-equipped building the heating-system was no problem. One of the members of our visiting panel asked why these garments were not left in the cloakroom, whereupon the teacher replied: 'If they leave 'em there, they'll be pinched.' We were a bit dismayed at this unashamed admission that in a school where the ratio of teachers to pupils was so favourable, children did not have the normal rights of security for their personal property. I could not help reflecting that they were suffering from a form of special deprivation, associated more with the school ethos than with the unfavourable circumstances of their neighbourhood.

Such experiences in schools as this cause me to wonder whether the School Handicap Score, referred to above, should not be extended in scope to include in its amalgam of social background variables what is probably the most important one of all—namely, the philosophy of learning subscribed to by the heads and staffs of schools and the resultant character of the teaching organization which operates within them. This I am sure has more effect upon the child than any other influence, but in recent years some schools seem more concerned with trimming their standards to the acceptable norm of their neighbourhood, rather than, as in past days, attempting to draw their deprived pupils up to a certain level of behaviour and achievement determined by themselves. This coming to terms with adverse environmental influences, instead of encouraging and inspiring disadvantaged children to improve themselves, is one of the by-products of the Dewey child-centred philosophy which has done so much to transform the purposeful, formal character of British schools into the flaccid and enervating cult of informality.

Nowhere do the sad effects of informality show up more starkly than in the case of children's reading, which it will be generally agreed is the most important subject on the school timetable, if in these days of freedom of curriculum, such a restrictive device as a timetable is any longer permissible. There is plenty of evidence to show that children are taking longer to read than they did in the early years of the century, when it was assumed that all, except a few retarded pupils, would be able to read on leaving the infant school for the junior department. Indeed, in the Report of the Consultative Committee of 1931, it stated that the task of the junior school should be to develop reading comprehension, since only a few 'backward' children would be in need of systematic instruction in reading mechanics after the age of seven. This optimistic pronouncement has been somewhat disproved by evidence from the National Child Development Study of 1972, quoted above, showing that 47% of 11,000 seven-year-olds needed the help in reading usually given at infant school level, and this is in line with the earlier research of Dr Joyce Morris in 1953, which indicated that among 3,000 first-year junior children, 45% needed the kind of teaching associated with the infant school, and 19% were virtual non-readers.

Although there is an obvious connection between the admitted slowing-down of the reading process and the general adoption of informal methods in British primary schools, advocates of these methods are very reluctant to admit the relationship. Yet the whole philosophy of child-centred schooling is based on Dewey's thesis that: 'Proficiency and learning come not from reading and listening but from action, from doing and experience.' If teachers go along with this view, it is not surprising that many infant and junior schools are dedicated to the encouragement of the happy noise and bustle of children finding out by discovery methods, rather than getting down to the humdrum labour of training pupils in the mechanics of reading in a quiet, orderly classroom situation. While Dewey cannot be blamed directly for the practice, it is significant that along with the introduction of activity methods, came the move towards look-and-say as the main method of teaching reading. Look-and-say claims to replace the tedium of learning letter-sounds by heart by offering whole words to be memorized by frequent association with pictures and objects. It is hoped that by teaching the child to respond to whole words rather than to attend to the separate parts of words, he will in time work out for himself the significance of the phoneme-grapheme relationship between letters and the sounds they represent. It is true that intelligent children are capable through look-and-say of teaching themselves to read, and this pleases the advocates of informal methods, but for children of average and below-average ability, the perception and identification of letter-sound relationships are far too complex, without constant prompting from teachers and persistent practice in the skills entailed.

Such children, and they are the bulk of the school population, cannot be left to themselves to pick up letter-sounds as they go along. They need systematic instruction in phonics from the beginning, and daily practice in the sounds which the letters make. It is true that there are some words which do not conform to a regular letter-sound rule, but these can be taught as whole words, and most children who have been taught phonically are not embarrassed by the exceptions which they encounter. Before the advent of look-and-say, teachers were prepared to spend much time on drilling children in the sounds of the letters, because they knew that only in this way could the majority of children learn to read. Such drills were certainly tedious and repetitive for teachers, often no doubt sheer drudgery, but the reward to both teacher and taught came when, through the mastery of phonics, any word, however unfamiliar, could be tackled, albeit haltingly, with certain hope of success. There was no unprofitable guessing from whole-word shapes as in look-and-say. Incidentally, drills in letter-sounds involving corporate chanting can be a source of delight to little children. They stir the primeval urge to rhythmic expression which is part of our heritage.

Now the teaching of reading through the sounds of the letters demands a great deal of teacher-direction and systematic training, and these features of learning are anathema to the child-centred theorists. There has been such emotional condemnation of didactic methods that any sign of teacher-direction and the inculcation of facts is condemned as authoritarian. It is out of keeping with the democratic conception of what school and life ought to be like in an ideal society. Yet in my view, teaching is most effective when it exercises firm control, and formality is essential in such a procedure.

In the last three decades the move to informal methods and the general use of look-and-say have had a great effect upon our schools, and I believe that the poor performance among the children from Social Classes 4 and 5, referred to in the I.L.E.A. and Aberdeen surveys quoted above, is directly attributable to this movement. Keith Gardner of Nottingham University School of Education has said: 'In the post-war infant school it has been considered slightly old-fashioned to teach reading at all. In the modern craze for child-centred education, reading has become something that is acquired—not taught.' After studying the early reading standards in the junior schools of one area, he found that while in 1961, 25% of 2,000 first-year pupils had not started to read, by 1967 the percentage had jumped to 40%.

A disturbing feature of the decline in reading standards among young children in recent years is that the new informal methods would appear to be particularly to the disadvantage of boys. It is noteworthy in this connection, that in the survey called *Roots of Reading* carried out for the N.F.E.R. by Cane and Smithers in 1971 we learn that in the twelve working-class infant departments which were studied, two years after entering (about age seven), 15% of the girls and 30% of the boys were still unable to read. An astute observer will no doubt ask why there should be twice as many boys as girls. Are boys less intelligent? Are they slower in development? Do they perhaps not respond as readily as girls to the new informal methods? The apologists for informality say that girls mature earlier than boys and this has been said so often recently that it is regarded as axiomatic. However, while it would be generally agreed that girls do mature earlier physically, this has not always been said about their intellectual growth. One of the manuals of instructions for Moray House Verbal Reasoning Tests, published by the University of Edinburgh, remarks on the higher mean scores achieved by girls over boys at age eleven. This is a general trend today and has to be taken into account in the allocation of girls and boys to grammar schools, the latter being able to 'pass' with lower scores than the former. In the words of the manual: 'During the war years a significant superiority of girls over boys developed in verbal intelligence-test performance, arising from the greater relaxation of discipline amongst boys. The effect is attributed to environment rather than native ability, as it did not show itself before the war.' The Plowden Report, while admitting that at the early age of seven, girls were found to be significantly better at reading than boys, does not attribute this to the new child-centred methods. This is understandable because Plowden advocates informal methods, but it is notable that in the context of the comparison between boys' and girls' reading attainments at seven, the Report notes, 'the lower the occupational status of the fathers, the poorer the reading attainment of the children'.

The modern tendency for boys to take longer over the reading process than girls confirms my view that informal methods in reading or in any other school activity are only suitable for those who do not need disciplinary pressure to work. Moreover, they have their worst effect upon children of below-average ability, and particularly those from disadvantaged environments. While it is possible for children of high ability from good social backgrounds to profit by less restrictive modes of learning than the somewhat rigid didactic procedures exercised in many schools in the past, for the great mass of our children the discipline, structure, system and purposeful direction of 'old-fashioned' formality are preferable. Children of low intelligence, without the backing of literate, ordered homes are at a particular disadvantage. They have little power of the application so necessary in the acquisition of reading skills, while discovering and picking things up incidentally are quite beyond their capacity. They have little self-motivation to learn so the teacher must compensate for this deficiency. They require a firm lead and delight in simple repetitive tasks when these are presented to them authoritatively. They have no respect for dissemblers. The 'smorgasbord' approach is not for them. They are used to being *told* what to do at home, often peremptorily and sometimes, alas, with a cuff. They expect teacher-direction at school and are bewildered when they do not receive it. It is not without significance that in the days of firm discipline and repetitive phonic techniques, we did not have this frightening number of non-readers. Children of low ability respond most enthusiastically to formal didactic methods which set out to instruct them, not to cajole them into learning. The implication of the increasing number of backward boys who, because they cannot read on entering the junior school, develop into truants, nuisances and even delinquents, is in my view related to the lack of system, structure and teacher-direction in many child-centred informal schools.

There has been little scientific inquiry into the comparative success in reading of formal and informal methods, but what there is seems to favour the former. In *The Challenge of Reading Failure*, a treatise commenting on Dr Morris's study of 7,409 children in 1953, Margaret Cox says quite unreservedly: 'Schools which used a formal, systematic approach to reading in the reception class, basing their instruction on a primer, seemed to produce better readers than the more permissive schools, and schools which undertook phonic instruction with five-year-olds produced better results, at least with children of average and below-average ability.' It is noteworthy that this commentator stresses that early phonics is good for those in the lower pool of ability. Unless these learn to read, they are the most likely to develop into the 'drop-outs' of our educational system.

In *Roots of Reading*, referred to above, an attempt was made to compare the relative success of twelve infant schools in deprived, lower working-class areas and to investigate the reasons for any variations. Data on the schools were collected by observers who were experienced teachers, and schools were classified in five degrees of success with reading. They were also classified in four degrees of 'teacher-direction'. The findings show clearly that there was in these twelve schools a close link between reading success and teacher-direction. This is how the researchers put it in their introductory chapter to the report:

A feature which may prove disturbing to progressive teachers—but will be taken all the more seriously for that—is that initial reading success does not prove to be associated with what are sometimes loosely considered 'progressive' methods. It is the schools where heads and teachers were 'superior' in their attitudes to parents, and where the learning programme was quite strongly teacher-directed that there was more success in the teaching of reading.

From the summary and discussion in the final chapter of the survey, the successful and unsuccessful schools are distinguished very pointedly:

Apart from having noisier surroundings, the unsuccessful schools did, in general, stand out as a group. The major difference—and it is one which forms a theme through our findings—was the lack of systematic instruction in the unsuccessful schools. There was considerable neglect of phonics (the sounds of individual letters and combinations of letters). There were few set periods of reading instruction, and in many classes the teachers waited for the children to manifest some interest in reading spontaneously before they attended to this subject. In the successful schools, reading instruction tended to be organized and recognizable from the start, and early phonic instruction was common. What distinguished the two groups of schools was not the warmth of atmosphere, nor the degree of concern for the children, which was manifest in most classrooms, but rather the extent to which the teacher exercised direct control over the children's learning. The unsuccessful schools favoured activity methods and creative work *at the expense* of organized learning. . . . The atmosphere in the successful schools, which was often strongly influenced by the headteachers' attitudes, was usually firmer and less indulgent than in the unsuccessful schools, but not to the extent of being harshly authoritarian. It transpired that all the unsuccessful schools were ones where there had not been much teacher-direction.

These extracts from the survey tend to demonstrate that early phonics, systematic instruction and definite teacher-direction are the prerequisites for success in reading, and although there was one exception to this general pattern, a child-centred school which was very successful, even here there was a certain amount of teacher-direction especially in organizing the learning of phonics. It is interesting to note that the successful schools were not disheartened by the very poor neighbourhoods in which they operated, nor were they depressed at the Social Handicap Scores of their pupils (if these were taken). We read:

The schools in the successful group, while heartily condemning what they saw as local social standards, were attempting to draw their pupils up to a certain level of achievement determined by themselves, whereas the unsuccessful group were inclined to lower their standards to what they believed to be an appropriate level.

This is the crux of the reading method argument. Good schools are not over-preoccupied with the social background of their pupils, but are prepared to battle on in the face of environmental difficulties, because their staffs are following clear objectives and have a declared rationale for their procedure. They are formal in spirit and therefore have a businesslike approach to their problems.

I think I have quoted enough from *Roots of Reading* to confirm my long-held conviction that formality in the teaching of this important subject—teacher-direction, systematic organization of class work, early phonics, firmness with pupils, work-orientation rather than child-centredness—is likely to be more effective as a foundation for reading success than the characteristics usually associated with the informal classroom. Now I do not suggest that because of the favourable features of formality adduced by Cane and Smithers, all informal methods should be condemned out of hand. There are child-centred schools where, under outstanding, dedicated heads and teachers, excellent results are achieved. The successful informal school referred to in the survey is such a one. But I am certain that because informality contains in itself certain fundamental weaknesses—lack of definition, lack of precision in development, lack of teacher-direction—and is therefore much too demanding for many of the teachers involved, it is not suitable for the great mass of heads and assistants, who are not able to cope with the unexpected problems it poses. In the words of Professor Stephen Wiseman:

Much harm has been done by the uncritical and thoughtless adoption of progressive methods by teachers with little grasp of the basic philosophy behind them; for weak teachers such methods may be beyond their capacity; they are perhaps safer with the formal methods which they *do* understand.

I believe that formality is essential in the day-to-day running of a school, because learning is a difficult operation demanding much conscious memorization, and this in turn requires effort and persistence from the learner. I do not believe that little children learning to read, or indeed any children learning anything, have the inbuilt motivation to make a success of the operation without teacher-direction and without pressure of some kind towards declared objectives. This is where the informal school is lacking. It does not provide these two important factors in the learning process.

Professor Peters in *Ethics and Education* gave an interesting and amusing picture of the modern progressive teacher, when he wrote: 'The traditional image of the teacher has been replaced in some quarters by that of the benign child-minder who keeps in the background and manipulates children by appealing to their interests. The teacher has identified himself with the attitudes of a consumer-orientated society.' I believe there is much in what Professor Peters says so wittily. Informal methods seem plausibly attractive, but their effectiveness is marred by their lack of structure and system, and of a sense of immediate and long-term purpose. They are too fuzzy and amorphous, and therefore I prefer teacher-directed formal procedures at all stages of children's schooling, particularly with beginning-reading.

The skill of being able to read is surely the most important accomplishment acquired by a child in his progress through school, and for this reason it must be planned precisely, presented gradually and methodically, and carried out with a purpose which only strict, formal methods are able to provide.

If a bold return to such purposeful methods were made in British primary schools, I think we should find that such a notion as the School Handicap Score would be rejected as an irrelevant absurdity.

Reading Instruction in America

GEORGE WEBER

Reading instruction is still in a state of flux in America, but many of the directions of change are now clear. Back in 1955, a book by Rudolf Flesch called *Why Johnny Can't Read* dropped like a bombshell on a complacent community of reading experts. Mr Flesch's thesis was that the whole-word approach to beginning reading instruction, used almost universally in the U.S.A. at that time, was wrong in theory and inferior in practice to a phonics approach. There were enough Johnnies having trouble with reading for the book to become an overnight sensation. The reading experts maintained that school reading attainments were satisfactory. When the public refused to agree, the experts shifted to saying that phonics were in fact being taught and, further, that Mr Flesch did not have expert's credentials.

Although Mr Flesch retired from the fray soon thereafter, for over a decade the argument continued. A few publishers got out instructional materials based on a phonics approach, but the publishers already established in the field held their ground.

Then in 1967 a book came from within the educational establishment that put an end to the theoretical arguments. Dr Jeanne Chall, a professor at Harvard, had reviewed a half-century of research on beginning reading instruction and concluded that the whole-word approach was indeed inferior to a phonics approach. The book *Learning to Read: The Great Debate* was sponsored by the prestigious Carnegie Corporation. The major textbook publishers, seeing the handwriting on the wall, began scrambling to change their materials. The reading experts covered themselves as well as they could and resurrected everything they had ever said in favour of phonics. Something as fundamental as the approach to beginning reading instruction could not be changed overnight, of course. New materials had to be produced. Teachers had to be reoriented. There was a natural resistance at the school level to changing what teachers had been doing for years. But change did take place slowly.

The pace of change was given an important boost in 1969, when the U.S. Commissioner of Education, the late James E. Allen Jr, started his right-to-read campaign. The significance of the event was that, for the first time, a federal Commissioner of Education acknowledged serious deficiencies in reading attainments. While sidestepping the question of method, Dr Allen characterized the large number of reading failures as 'a reproach to all of us' in education and called the situation in reading instruction 'inexcusable' and 'intolerable'. Among the salient facts that he cited was that about half of the nation's unemployed young people between the ages of sixteen and twenty-one were functionally illiterate.

While the theoretical argument has been settled since 1967, the change at the classroom level from a whole-word approach to a phonics approach is still under way. Instructional materials, teaching procedures, and teacher training typically have many vestiges of the whole-word approach, even though all textbook publishers, schools, teachers, and teacher training institutions now say they are using phonics.

In America, formal reading instruction is rarely begun in the first year of school, kindergarten, which is for five-year-olds. Many communities still do not have kindergartens in the public (tax-supported) schools, and no state requires kindergarten attendance. In the first three grades, for children six to eight, the most popular programme still is the whole-word approach. But today it usually involves either supplemental phonics materials or textbooks that have been updated by having some phonics added. These programmes still have relatively limited vocabularies, chosen on the basis of presumed frequency of the words in spoken language, and still utilize some of the old techniques of identifying new words.

The phonics-approach programmes are still in the minority and can be divided into four categories. The most common are sometimes called 'linguistic' and teach phonics principles by way of 'word patterns': Dan, fan, pan. There is little or no instruction of the sounds in isolation. A second type—what might be called pure phonics—teaches the letter-sounds in isolation. A third type uses word patterns but in a programmed format so that each child can proceed at his own pace. A final type is the one using special orthography. The only important programme of this type is the initial teaching alphabet, imported from England in 1964. Its use is very limited and in recent years has not grown. All of these phonics-approach programmes introduce words on the basis of phonics principles. At the end of a year or so, the vocabularies used are typically far larger than in the whole-word programmes.

Certainly, the schools are using a lot more phonics than they did nineteen years ago, when Flesch's book appeared.

The outlook is for a continued drift toward more phonics and more use of phonics-approach programmes. Perhaps ten years from now, almost all schools will be using phonics-approach programmes and the cycle of change will be complete.

About 15% of America's young adults are functionally illiterate. Although almost all of these can read a little, and are therefore called literate by the national Census Bureau, they cannot read well enough to meet the minimum daily demands of a complex modern society. They cannot read an application for a driver's licence, for example, or a popular newspaper. As beginning reading instruction continues to improve, this percentage will fall.

With the most important theoretical questions about beginning reading settled, reading research has begun to turn to questions having to do with reading beyond the beginning level. Of the poor readers in the upper grades and secondary schools, what proportion have mastered the mechanics of reading (decoding) but lack the vocabulary, grammar, logic, and general information to read at higher levels? Once decoding is mastered, how should formal reading instruction proceed to attain these other skills? If children succeed in the early stages of reading, is their motivation adequate to enable them to gain higher levels of reading? Do we need more attention to teaching children, particularly those from homes where little or no reading is done by adults, to want to read? If such questions can be answered, further progress in reading accomplishments can be made. Just how important these matters are may not be clear until beginning reading instruction improves to the point where almost all nine-year-olds have mastered the mechanics of reading.

Progressivism and the Content of Education

G. H. BANTOCK

Progressivism is often regarded primarily—and indeed exclusively—as a methodology, a new way of accomplishing the traditional aims of cultural transmission by exploiting psychological discoveries concerning optimum learning conditions. Indeed, as an umbrella term it covers so many meanings that there are certainly some people who would term themselves 'progressives' and whose aim is simply to achieve superior standards in the traditional curriculum by new means.

But no serious consideration of the practice of many of our 'progressives' nor of the long history, stretching from at least the eighteenth century, of the development of 'progressive' ideas could avoid the truth that progressivism, both traditionally and contemporaneously, has very serious implications for the content of education. As usual, the situation can be more easily and comprehensively understood if I start by examining the inferences to be drawn from an examination of the work of two men both of whom have been regarded as the 'father' of progressive education and both of whom have contributed to a developing ambivalence over the content of education.[1] Briefly Rousseau, in the education of the younger Emile (in that part of *Emile* which has exerted most influence subsequently), asserted the superiority of nature to culture; John Dewey affirmed the claims of community in preference to the restrictions, as he saw them, of the academic. Both views involve versions of primitivism and both have had repercussions on our views of curriculum.

The most superficial reading of *Emile* will make clear its author's attachment to the concept of 'Nature'; but a moment's thought will also make it clear that the idea of nature is being used in a number of different ways. Two are important for my theme. A form of simple, comparatively primitive (*not* savage) life becomes the norm to be achieved in which the child is to accomplish self-regulation and self-direction in a comparatively egalitarian rural community—this constitutes a more 'natural' form of existence than that to be found in towns and courts.

Furthermore human development is governed by 'natural' laws analogous to those discovered to be controlling the material environment. At times Rousseau seems to suggest that these laws assert themselves in purely endogenous terms: 'The mind should be left undisturbed until its faculties have developed.' Hence the apparent lifting of all cultural restraints. At other times it is appreciated that 'nature' can be assisted by human intervention: 'His sense experiences are the raw material of thought: they should therefore be presented to him in fitting order.' This quotation not only implies the tutor's active interference but points to the *kind* of learning that Rousseau wishes to encourage. In reaction against the verbalism of Renaissance humanism Rousseau asserts the importance of 'things' over 'words'. In brief the aim is to turn the child into a discoverer, learning to correlate phenomena and acquire technical skills in a way which implies a pre-scientific rather than a humanistic content. Symptomatically Rousseau banishes books ('the scourge of childhood') except *Robinson Crusoe*—the handyman's guide to self-sufficiency. The study of the social and emotional arts is to be delayed until adolescence—by which time the child will have been protected against the ravages of social corruption and concessions may be made to social life. The essence of the Emilean experience lies in an attempt to transcend history—history interpreted as the influences of family and the traditional humanistic culture of Europe—though a limited technical competence (which, of course, must have a social origin) is to be preserved. In place of ordered curriculum is substituted, as organizing principles, the shifting and sporadic demands of daily living—the *practical* exigencies of daily life—and such coherence as the environmental tinkerings of the tutor can indirectly introduce. In so far as it is possible to detect any structure in this early education it lies in the production of technico-scientific man; but the text is as liberally scattered with repudiations as it is with affirmations: 'Everyone knows that the learned societies of Europe are mere schools of falsehood, and there are assuredly more mistaken notions in the Academy of Sciences than in a whole tribe of American Indians.' It is

---

[1] I argued the validity of this method of historical exegesis in my contribution to *Black Paper Two*, on discovery methods.

not surprising that, some years ago, in a radio talk, Sir Isaiah Berlin described Rousseau as the 'first militant low brow in history'.

And of course there are strong egalitarian overtones in this education: 'Nature's characters alone are ineffaceable, and nature makes neither the prince, the rich man nor the nobleman'—the normative overtones rarely absent from Rousseau's use of the concept of Nature are brought into play in order to persuade in a way which would cause a modern geneticist to raise his eyebrows at the implication intended. The same sleight of hand is used to blur reaction to the evaluative implications of 'needs' in the statement: 'natural needs are the same to all.' As a creative principle 'Nature' (among other things) implies a degree of homogenization which contributed greatly to the Enlightenment's anti-hierarchical stance and has entered into the fundamentals of political thinking down to our own day.

From here the story can be taken up by John Dewey. Dewey lies uneasily between a liberal, individualized past and a collectivist, homogenized future. Two elements in his thinking continue Rousseau's line of thought—his instrumentalism and his concern for 'democracy'. As an Instrumentalist, Dewey, like Rousseau, saw knowledge as something for use, as an 'instrument' in the more effective control of the environment to serve man's purposes; it involved 'a change from knowing as aesthetic enjoyment of the properties of nature regarded as a work of divine art, to knowing as a means of secular control'. This involved a development of Rousseau's principle of learning from the environment in order to cope with the exigencies of daily life: 'mere amassing of information apart from the direct interests of life makes mind wooden', he writes, in his own wooden way. And so he becomes the father (as Rousseau was the grandfather) of the 'project', the real life situation as the organizing principle in terms of which the logical development of subject matter is 'psychologized' (Dewey's word) for the purpose of making it meaningful: 'The school must represent present life—life as real and vital to the child as that which he carries on in the home, in the neighbourhood, or in the playground.' The modern British primary school has discovered one of its founding fathers.

But just as significant is his concern for 'democracy'. By 'democracy' Dewey implied more than a form of government: in essence it constituted a form of community relationship—and, most important for its implications for curriculum, invaded the very concept of 'meaning' itself. It was not only a question of 'associated living' and 'freer interaction between social groups'; it was also a matter of the homogenization of significance in communication. William Blake (not exactly an Establishment figure) had reasserted the significance of individual experience, as against the unifying tendencies of the philosophy of the Enlightenment, with its conception of an abstract 'humanity' manifest as homogenized units, with his assertion 'A fool *sees* not the same tree that a wise man sees' (my italics); in contradistinction Dewey defines his social groups in terms of each individual's acceptance of a common *meaning*: 'to have the same ideas about things which others have, to be like-minded with them, and thus to be really members of a social group, is to attach the same meanings to things and to acts which others attach.' For Dewey it is the *social* situation which provides the great tool of the educator: 'In social situations the young have to refer their way of acting to what others are doing and make it fit in. This directs their action to a common result, and gives an understanding common to the participants. For all *mean* the same thing, even when performing different acts.' This common understanding of the means and ends of action is the essence of social control. However unwittingly—and one must surely acquit Dewey of *intent*—

he has taken a long step on the road to George Orwell's *1984*, where all meaning is the same meaning, imposed by the Party ('War is Peace, Freedom is Slavery, Ignorance is Strength').

In essence we have here the fundamental *social* argument in favour of comprehensive schooling—its putative power as an instrument of social cohesion and even control. A powerful element in the comprehensive lobby sees it as a vehicle of social justice and as a means of doing away with what is regarded as a damaging 'divisiveness' in our society. For such people equality of *opportunity* is not enough—we should seek (if necessary by 'positive discrimination' in favour of the under-achiever[2]), equality of *outcome*. Dewey's views on 'meaning' represent the ultimate in that direction.

So far I have alluded briefly and in general terms to the implications of these views of the founding fathers of progressivism for the content of education. It is now necessary to spell these hints out in much greater detail. Before I do so, however, there is one general point of great importance, concerning the whole orientation of the traditional education vis-à-vis the progressive.

Clearly the content of education over the last two thousand years has altered significantly—though for an astonishingly long period classical studies formed the staple diet. Nevertheless, the enterprise was informed, throughout this period, by conceptions of excellence, by the search for perfection, by the search for the Idea in its highest form. Whether the aim is to produce the Philosopher-King (Plato), the Orator (Quintilian) or the Courtier (Castiglione)—all, incidentally, intended to take an *active* part in affairs—in each case it is such conception of the Ideal type as we can arrive at which exercises the controlling influence over the content of their education: 'It would be absurd to deny that a philosopher is a lover of truth and reality; or that his nature, as we have described it, is allied to perfection' (Plato). 'The Orator whom we are educating is the perfect orator, who can only be a good man' (Quintilian). 'I would like our game this evening to be this: that one of us should be chosen and given the task of depicting in words a perfect courtier' (Castiglione); and the tradition was carried on into the nineteenth century by Cardinal Newman and others. It is this 'vision of greatness'—in Whitehead's phrase—which has informed the determination of curriculum in the past; and as the social role aimed at has been conceived of in its perfection, so the contributory activities, whether mental or physical, have been conceived of in their own specific perfections. The new humanist concern of the Renaissance with letters (as well as physical prowess) which changed the entire character of the European aristocracy, was informed by qualitative considerations; and those qualitative considerations derived from the excellences implicit in the revived disciplines themselves—so that, for instance, as a matter of method, the emphasis was often on *imitation* (of the best models, derived from classical antiquity); and usefulness—which undoubtedly existed as a value, for ultimately this was an education for action—was to be informed by an antecedent liberalization. As Sir Thomas Elyot put it: 'pure and excellent learning, if it be translated to another study of a more gross quality vanisheth and cometh to nothing.' What he meant is that liberal understanding should precede technical know-how; in this way the accidental events of everyday life will be encountered by a mind already prepared to assess such accidents by reference to philosophic principle and contextual significance.

[2] This, indeed, is official policy: 'When I talk about equality, I mean more than the equality of opportunity. . . . Equality entails an element of positive discrimination in favour of disadvantaged children.' Mr R. Prentice, quoted in *The Times*, 5 August 1974.

This tradition still informs the behaviour of our grammar school and university education. I once listened to a fascinating discussion, on a B.Ed. board of studies, between a college of education head of department and a professor of French in the university. The college approach was practical—teach them how to speak French; the professor argued that there was no virtue simply in teaching students how to speak French—there were fifty million Frenchmen who could do that but few of them had anything to say worth listening to: the emphasis must be on language at its best—i.e. the literature of the country. The accidental demands of everyday life could be met subsequently from a mind richly stored with a language used in its most discriminating way.

But the principle behind the progressive view of the curriculum is essentially that of the accidental; Rousseau wishes for an education that will be *immediately* useful— 'Life is the trade I would teach him'—and the motivating force is provided by the incidents of daily existence—the activities of the gardener, a conjurer at a fair, a note from Emile's parents, an attempt to gather the cherries from the tree in the garden. Clearly Rousseau is still sustained by the Christian-humanist tradition—'life' for him would not have included the activities of a Fagin—but his approach involved no ordered attempt to convey the structures of knowledge in a coherent fashion. And the same is true of the modern British primary school in its more progressive guise. Temporary *interest* and immediate *need* are the guiding principles implicit in the attempt to 'psychologize' learning; for the emphasis on motivation and endogenous development too easily degenerate into a magpie curriculum of bits and pieces, unrelated and ephemeral. In the interests of a temporary *relevance* a more permanent and deeper comprehension is often sacrificed.

Let us, with this indictment in mind, consider the current fashion for the interdisciplinary. Subject divisions are often dismissed as 'artificial' largely on the grounds that everyday living constantly involves the crossing and re-crossing of subject boundaries and 'life as real as the home or the playground' is the object of our endeavour. But of course our 'living' is only interdisciplinary, as it were, in our moments of inattention and of imperfect consciousness. As soon as we focus our attention, seek to transcend the largely mindless play of our daily existence, we enter an essentially specialized world. That building is a certain shape—what is the meaning of that shape, of the way the space has been deployed? Only a knowledge of architecture in its central concern with mass, space and line can provide the answer.[3] A study of 'Our Town' (a popular subject) involves historical, economic, geographical features (among others) which, to take on significance beyond the most superficial, imply some degree of inwardness with the concepts and development of the various subject fields involved; otherwise all that occurs is a meaningless copying from books and authorities (a not infrequent manifestation, it can be said), in undifferentiated enthusiasm.

The error implicit in an exclusive diet of this sort of thing lies in its haphazardness—and its subjectivity. It is to see the world as an appendage of self without a meaning to be sought or guessed at apart from the meaning temporarily assigned in relation to one's immediate interests; it marks a failure to appreciate the integrity of the other, of what lies outside the self. All action, of course, is personal action and depends in the last resort on the responsibility of the self.

[3] Indeed, as a protest against the blurring of specific *architectural* concerns by extraneous considerations of a technical, aesthetic or historical nature relevant to the wider society cf. Geoffrey Scott's study *The Architecture of Humanism*, a classic statement of a deterioration of taste which results from the homogenization of elements more properly to be distinguished.

But that self, to be wisely formed, must display some humility before other selves and their behaviour, which is what is implied by a culture, and which it is the business of education to transmit. The danger of an education based totally on imitation is, of course, atrophy; the danger of an education which is based on novelty, the 'dominance of the foreground' as Santayana puts it, and immediacy, is instability and parochialism, with the eccentricities and worse which accompany these conditions.

As a child I was brought up in a way which would currently seem barbaric—almost exclusively on rote learning. Between the ages of five and ten I learnt chunks of the Bible, gobbets of Shakespeare, fifty spelling words a week, the names of the kings and queens of England and the chief battles, the names of county towns, chief manufactures, capes, bays, isthmuses, rivers—sometimes in blank incomprehension. ('Never tell a child what he cannot understand', advised Rousseau.) I have forgotten practically all of this—but I have not forgotten the lesson it implied: that the world, physical and cultural, existed as an entity apart from myself and that if I wished to learn about it I must come to terms with its existence. The famous remark in the Primary School Report of 1931 perpetuates a false dichotomy: 'the curriculum is to be thought of in terms of activity and experience rather than of knowledge to be acquired and facts to be stored.' Knowledge, as I have tried to indicate above, is an essential part of experience: mind is selective and only focuses meaningfully on what it already knows about. Otherwise it is left to the blankness of 'What is that?'—the cry of blank incomprehension.

I am far from saying that occasional projects of an interdisciplinary nature should not be undertaken; but it should be realized that even their value as stimuli is limited to an essentially restricted attraction unless the ephemeral configurations of daily existence are informed by a deeper understanding of the parts which are brought into temporary contiguity in the project—and which have been studied as 'subjects'. For 'subjects' are precisely ways in which the incoherence of everyday experience is made meaningful, broken down into its constituent elements and illumined by study in depth. Such study is not to be dismissed as artificial but as an essential element in that very comprehension of the foreground the progressives wish to promote.

Furthermore, it is a psychological error to think that even young children are attracted only by the immediate— the assumption being that their world is bound in by the scope of their sense experiences. In contradistinction to Rousseau's analysis of La Fontaine's fable of the Fox and the Crow, with its emphasis on the scientific inaccuracy of the elements of the fable, Coleridge urged the need for the remote and the imaginative:

> For from my early reading of fairy tales and genii, &c., &c., my mind had been habituated *to the Vast*, and I never regarded *my senses* in any way as the criteria of my belief. I regulated all my creeds by my conceptions, not by my *sight*, even at that age. . . . I have known some who have been *rationally* educated, as it is styled. They were marked by a microscopic acuteness, but when they looked at great things, all became a blank and they saw nothing, and denied (very illogically) that anything could be seen. . . .

The theory behind a recent set of readers for young children, Leila Berg's *Nippers*, is that children appreciate the familiar and are at home among the actualities of language and sights assumed to belong to their everyday life. But many find it embarrassing to read out loud: 'Cor don't it pong', or are bored with the mundaneness. They much prefer the 'unreality' of Sheila McCullogh's *The Three Pirates* or Dr Seuss's *A Cat in the Hat*.

The argument in favour of the exploitation of the immediate and the everyday in the name of stimulation and interest would seem to be most compelling at the younger ages, when children are arguably, in the terminology of Piaget, at the level of 'concrete operations' and need the stimulus of the actual. What I have tried to show is that even at this age such principles governing the content of education should be treated with some caution as at best limited guides—limited both in the way in which sense experience itself is a limited principle to guide curricular choice and also in the way in which this is meaningless unless it is enforced by comprehension of significance—and significance is not a characteristic of surface.

Inevitably, with this analysis of immediacy and relevance, we have strayed into the domain of Dewey. Dewey, as I have said, sees knowledge as power, a tool for the active reconstruction of the environment. To that extent he carries on Rousseau's emphasis derived from his admiration for Robinson Crusoe. But Dewey introduces another note which is of the greatest significance for our present-day practices. Rousseau's Emile, as a young child, is of intent conceived of as an isolate, learning the self-sufficiency which would make him independent of any specific social arrangement. Dewey places his emphasis on environmental rearrangement within a very specific framework—the democratic; and as we have seen above, his conception of the democratic has very serious consequences for the range of meaning he finds it desirable to transmit.

His concern for cultural homogenization as an essential element in social democratic consensus and harmonization leads him to value-considerations which have deeply affected current arguments concerning, and practice within, the comprehensive school. He has both emphasized the primary value of the experiences open to the widest number and at the same time denied the possibility of any discrimination on the grounds of intrinsic value as between different areas of subject matter. Thus he asserts that 'the curriculum must be planned with reference to placing essentials first, and refinements second. The things which are socially most fundamental, that is, which have to do with the experiences in which the widest groups share, are the essentials.' At the same time he also asserts that:

> We cannot establish a hierarchy of values among studies. It is futile to attempt to arrange them in an order, beginning with one being least worth and going on to that of maximum value. In so far as any study has a unique or irreplaceable function, in so far as it makes a characteristic enrichment of life, its worth is intrinsic or incomparable.

The contradiction between 'first' and 'second' in the first quotation vis-à-vis the categorical refusal in the second to arrange in any order hardly requires comment. Yet it is precisely this covert approach of mediocritization combined with an overt uncertainty about value discriminations which is beginning to characterize comprehensive education in this country today.

The comprehensive undertaking, it must be understood, is the product of two contrary impulses, one seeking greater equality of *opportunity*, the other implying greater equality of *outcome*. Inefficiencies of selection at 11 + (and, despite the care taken, no-one can refuse to admit such inefficiencies, though in the opinion of the National Foundation for Educational Research they can be reduced to about 10% of wrong placements) led to the belief that there was a hidden reservoir of talent currently depressed by the low status of the secondary modern school. Remove the stigma of that institution by grouping all in the same school and late developers would blossom, anomalies concerning percentage allocations to grammar schools would be ironed out, and a more equal opportunity would be afforded to all to become unequal. But there is a powerful body of comprehensive opinion which emphasized the social, 'democratic' implications of the single school. The mixture of different social classes within the same institution would promote mutual understanding and sympathy. This necessitated the submission of all to a similar regimen or, in order to allow for the individual differences for learning which undoubtedly manifest themselves, promoted a value relativism, reminiscent of Dewey's refusal to discriminate between activities, which allocated an equivalent worth to the university scholar and the champion swimmer. (That animals can swim but cannot operate within human symbolic systems, of course, escaped notice.) But the long-range effort was to promote equality of *outcome*, on the grounds that current deficiencies among certain sections of the school population were due, not to 'innate' or irreducible differences of ability but the accident of family background and impoverished upbringing. The 'deprivation' industry got under way—but more of this later.

This contradiction implicit in the main aims behind the comprehensive 'philosophy' has had specific implications for the content of education. There has first been the attempt to impose a common core curriculum on all for the first one, two or three years. This has led to such monstrosities as the teaching of French (or German) to those who are barely literate in their own language; alternatively the dropping of early Latin for the capable. There has been the organizational device of non-streaming necessitating individual assignments and the boredom which, for some children, has resulted in the substitution of a work-card for the active stimulus of the teacher's exposition in a competitive class situation. But above all, there has been the polarization of school ethos—between those who, in general, see the function of the school as primarily academic and those who see it as largely socialization.[4] In most comprehensive schools there is some degree of such polarization among the staff, which results in a blurred image of what the school is intended to be about. But at times it results in schools which are either predominantly meritocratic or socially oriented in nature. The point can be illustrated by reference to two schools of which a good deal has recently appeared in the press. Highbury Grove School, about which controversy has arisen concerning the replacement of the former headmaster, Dr Rhodes Boyson, is a highly meritocratic institution where the emphasis is on disciplined, structured learning and achievement in examination terms. I have visited the school myself on several occasions during Dr Boyson's headmastership. Discipline was firm but cheerful; attention was paid to social matters but the aim of the headmaster was undisguisedly and unashamedly academic in the sense that learning took first priority. The snide comments of a few staff members since his departure have shown that unanimity did not necessarily reign among the staff concerning the ethos of the school; but while he was in control the work atmosphere of the school was unmistakable to the most casual visitor. The school was heavily oversubscribed by would-be pupils, as is indicated by the title of Dr Boyson's recent book, *Oversubscribed: The Story of Highbury Grove* (1974).

Leicestershire has the first fully comprehensive system in

---

[4] A perfect example of such confusion comes to hand in an article by Dr Briault, Chief Education Officer for Inner London Education Authority, seeking to defend comprehensive schools from an attack by Mr Ronald Butt. He at once advocates 'a common culture', necessary to avoid 'a fragmented adult society of groups who find it difficult to communicate with one another' in the best Dewey tradition and at the same time a 'liberal' fragmentation implicit in a passionately stated concern 'to provide for and to meet the needs of every individual as an individual' (*The Times*, 25 July 1974).

the country; and several of its upper schools have attracted considerable public attention. Here one has to rely neither on possibly biased newspaper reports nor personal impression; for Countesthorpe College, on the outskirts of Leicester, has received a dispassionate sociological examination by Professor G. Bernbaum of the University of Leicester School of Education.[5] The aims of the first headmaster, Mr McMullen, are discussed at some length, and it becomes clear that a major concept in his thinking was that of 'relevance'; furthermore his strange confusion of liberal individualism and group corporate aims is highly reminiscent of the Deweyan dilemma adumbrated above. But perhaps the most significant findings relate to the orientation of the staff recruited. Here is a school where the instrumental aims (i.e. academic achievement) are underrated at the expense of the expressive (i.e. socialization). The attitude of a 'large number' of the staff

. . . towards the academic work of the school is ambiguous. It has already been shown that the largest staff choice for the most important innovation (45%) is in the area of greater equality in social relations between staff and children. It has been shown, also, that this aspect of the school gives most staff their greatest satisfaction. Moreover, when the teachers were given a list of 12 items by means of which the influence of the school would make itself felt and asked to say whether the item was likely to be 'Highly Important', 'Moderately Important', or 'Not Important', the two items which received the highest number of 'Highly Important' rulings were:
  (i) Visible improvements in pupils' social adjustment.
  (ii) Visible improvements in the community's involvement in the school.
Both of these are clearly in the expressive area. Significantly, also, visible improvement in pupils' academic achievement was placed eleventh out of twelve in the 'Highly Important' column.[6]

The graduate teachers tend to emphasize academic goals; the non-graduates opt for relationships and socialization; Countesthorpe is not the only school where similar polarizations take place; 'socialization' in all its vagueness and undemanding quality is the perfect bogey hole for the academically under-achieving staff member who is scared of the demands of the brighter children in the all-capacity school.

What, in fact, does 'socialization' imply in terms of curriculum content? Key concepts again tend to be 'relevance' and the 'interdisciplinary'; for one development within the comprehensive school, faced with an indigestible diversity of talent and the homogenizing tendencies implicit in the notion of socialization with its emphasis (albeit unconscious) on equality of outcome, has been the infiltration of progressive approaches at the secondary level; and the same criticisms previously offered concerning the revised content of primary school work apply with even greater force at the secondary level—at least where able children are concerned; for as the capacity for abstraction increases, the excuse of concreteness no longer applies with the same force. Those who are ready for study in depth no longer require the titillations of immediacy as motivation.

As an example, let us see how 'relevance' works in relation to the teaching of a specific subject at secondary level —English. The traditional emphasis stressed, among other factors, the centrality of literature; it was not always well taught, but it constituted an attempt to grapple with the language at its finest point of excellence. Recently the centrality of literature has been under attack. Drama has become spontaneous, 'active' drama revealing too often little other than the linguistic and histrionic impoverishment of the children creating it. Such literature as has survived has become mainly contemporary and often radical, necessitating in many cases the study of inferior texts [7] which an earlier age would have, at best, prescribed for private reading. The progressive emphasis on either endogenous creativity (undisciplined by any inwardness with the language of greatness) or social relevance (applying the human reductiveness characteristic of much of the contemporary) has replaced an earlier concern for quality. Where language is concerned, middle-class speech structures are being attacked in favour of 'everyday' speech. 'A new respect for everyday language is needed', writes Miss Nancy Martin in one of a series of articles published in *The Times Educational Supplement* (17 May 1974), the net effect of which (despite occasional disclaimers) is to deprecate the structures of educated speech in favour of the putative superior 'expressiveness' of the everyday. One does not need to be wedded to the turgidity of *some* school writing not to see the dangers of this—with its implied cult of an unregenerate and surface expressiveness.[8] It is the same attitude that defends the introduction of 'pop' into the schools.

And yet one can see that the school is in a genuine dilemma, posed in part by the incompatibility of its aims; and this confusion is itself the outcome of an unwillingness to face up to the fact that education, *by its very nature, is socially divisive.* To educate is to transmit meaning; and the development of meaning implies the ability to make finer and finer discriminations in a language of ever-increasing complexity and precision. For whatever reason (historical or genetic) only some can grasp this refined meaning; and *neither genetic make-up nor history can be much transcended,* so that whether inhibiting factors are hereditary or environmental (which is inescapably historical) is irrelevant. The theoretical confusion implied by the contradictory arguments used to justify comprehensivization reveals a deep confusion in our society of liberal versus collectivist valuations which far transcends their deployment within the educational system. The effects on that system, however, simply mean that for the uncertainties of selection have been substituted the uncertainties of secondary school ethos; and for the wickedness of coaching has been substituted the reprehensibleness of house-moving into the 'better' catchment areas, i.e. those areas within which the schools seek primarily to fulfil their instrumental function of promoting academic learning, and produce good results.

The point is that under the present comprehensive system the incoherence of its aims puts at risk either the

[7] Usually, one charitably assumes, because they are supposed to introduce a note of social 'realism' to children who are too young and inexperienced to relate the squalor revealed in all its degradation to a balanced view of human potential.

[8] The theoretical justification for this sort of approach is supplied by such writers as William Labov (cf. 'The Logic of Non-standard English' reprinted in *Tinker, Tailor . . . The Myth of Cultural Deprivation*, ed. Nell Keddie). Labov seeks to defend N.N.E. (non-standard Negro English) against 'middle-class' imputations of inadequacy. In her introduction Miss Keddie draws attention to the implications of this for the imputed inadequacies of working-class speech in this country. Cf. also Chris Searle, *This New Season*, where he finds working-class speech superior: 'The teacher of English must stand up and affirm the working-class loyalties of the language that his students speak' (p. 136). Mr Searle's dilemma is a genuine one; his solution is unacceptable because he imprisons himself in the categories of class when as an English teacher he should be concerned simply with quality—which transcends class.

[5] Cf. 'Countesthorpe College, Leicester, United Kingdom' in *Case Studies of Educational Innovation III At School Level* (O.E.C.D. 1973). The general ethos of the school seems to have altered only marginally since the time the survey was carried out.
[6] Cf. op. cit. p. 74.

ablest or the lowest achievers. It also, conceivably, mediocritizes still further the mediocre. For the prime error arises out of having regarded the undoubted stresses within the old system as organizational rather than what they irrefutably are—cultural. There are at last signs that this point is being taken; but though the dilemma is being correctly diagnosed, the solutions offered are unacceptable. What I am referring to represents, in theoretical terms, the latest effort to resolve the dilemma implicit in the attempt to transmit an essentially élite curriculum to a total population—and it comes from the radical left, as a development beyond traditional progressivism. It has been hinted at in my remarks on the teaching of English earlier.

Two strands of thought have gone to stimulate the new recognition: the appreciation of a diversity of linguistic codes within the school community and the realization of the comparatively weak cultural authority of the school vis-à-vis the home. It is part of the conventional wisdom of our times that the working classes speak a 'restricted' code and the middle classes an 'elaborated' one—and no refinements of the Bernsteinian thesis seem to destroy this view of a broad, class-based differentiation. The element of truth in the diagnosis obviously gives grave offence to those who see in the concept of 'restricted' an implied slur on the working classes who have, in our century, become the focal point of those regressive instincts of the sophisticated classes who in other days projected their desire for a simplified form of existence into a pastoral setting. Professor Bernstein himself has sought to remove any hint of stigma by arguing that the working classes have a potential for elaboration and at the same time possess a form of language which has its own validity and richness.[9] The radicals have seized on this hint and at the same time accepted implicitly the superior socializing power of the home by formulating the solution of the alternative culture.

Hence the current deprecation of middle-class culture as a form of social tyranny intended to keep 'the poor in their place', and the search for 'validity' elsewhere. There is, as Mr Brian Jackson, in defending working-class life, is partly correct in thinking: '. . . some awakening sense that main-stream working-class life is a culture the schools are not in dialogue with, a style of life as valid as any other.' The word 'valid' in this context, of course, receives its justification from an attitude of mind of which Dewey's refusal to make discriminations of value as between various subjects is symptomatic. And the bankruptcy of the claim becomes apparent when attempts are made to define more precisely what this working-class culture consists of. Mr Colin McInnes in a recent number of *The Times Educational Supplement* (5 October 1973) found it in such activities as horse and dog racing, bingo, variety, pop: the only areas with any potential that he mentions are gardening and 'do-it-yourself' hobbies, neither of which is by any means exclusive to the working classes. Mr Jackson himself has exchanged an earlier enthusiasm for brass bands and pigeon fancying for even more dubious activities:

> Spend any time in a decaying back street, and you'll see how important television or football pools are. Or chalking on walls. Or pulling a motor bike to pieces. Or a group of girls dolling up each other's hair. Why isn't the education service there, putting on children's chalking competitions, building runnable cars out of junk, dress making, street theatre, 'Holiday at Home' weeks?[10]

[9] Cf. 'Education Cannot Compensate for Society', *New Society*, 28 February 1970.

[10] In 'How the poorest live: education', *New Society*, 1 February 1973, p. 230.

Behind this notion, of course, lies the exploitation by radical sociologists of the recent revived interest in the sociology of know-

Could the attempt to build a curriculum on the actual and the incidental be pushed any further? The mind boggles at the thought of the attempt to find significance in a course on graffiti; the state of many school walls and the obscenities which there appear might justify some attention in this area, though not quite in Mr Jackson's terms.

Indeed, it is only possible to pretend that the working classes today have a culture if one juggles with the meaning of the word culture. Clearly, if it is interpreted in its anthropological sense as a way of life, the working classes can be said to have a distinctive life-style; but in its evaluative sense, the old folk-culture has been destroyed by industrialization; and there are no longer elements in working-class life as such which could require the sort of structured approach implicit in the notion of schooling. The danger is that the homogenizing tendencies implicit in the social arguments for comprehensive education will trivialize the traditional curriculum without finding an alternative suited to the needs of the low-achievers.[11]

We are now perhaps in a position to see the contemporary dangers posed historically by Rousseau's insistence on nature and Dewey's on socialization. Both constitute forms of threat to the traditional culture by way of an over-attention to the trivia of daily existence—whether social or 'natural'; both imply the immediate, the foreground, an attenuated sense of relevance as the criterion of judgment; both imply a restless, unfocused attention, failing to appreciate that each manifestation of daily life, properly conceived, belongs to a context which transcends the immediate, finds its meaning only in a memory which is not present or a configuration which transcends the incidental. The essential contrast between the old and the new education can be expressed in this way. The old, which, granted, has evolved over the centuries since the time when Erasmus exclaimed that everything worth knowing was contained in the literature of Greece and Rome, has been based on the autonomy of the culture as something to be come to terms with, submitted to and grappled with in its own terms; the new, whether at the behest of 'Nature' or the collectivity, implies all the restrictiveness of immediate relevance; this 'relevance' and its implications for content, may be controlled either by the accidents of personal viewpoint and immediate whim or the homogenization implied by majority commitment. The current thinness of much

ledge. Knowledge is seen as a means of social control; as a social and historical product reflecting simply the interests of the dominant classes. It is not possible to argue the superiority of one cultural form to another. Cf. *Knowledge and Control*, ed. M. F. D. Young, 1971. Cf. a comprehensive school headmaster (quoted in *The Times Educational Supplement*, 7 June 1974) on teachers who cause difficulties; among them 'those imbued with newer notions about repressive middle-class culture. These come out of college with *Knowledge and Control* in the bloodstream. They assume that to get on with working-class children you must pretend to be working class. But children do not want you to play a patronizing role.'

[11] 'At Harfurley [High School, a comprehensive for 1,100 girls in north-east Manchester] the academic groups have complained at not having the same opportunities [as less able groups]. . . . This flattering jealousy is getting a special boost from the experimental 'charm course' (hair-dressing, clothes, make-up, poise, diet, etc.). . . . The phenomenon was already observable during the North-West project trials [for R.S.L.A. pupils]. . . . "There was quite a feeling all through the trials by the more able children that they were being deprived"' ('Business as Usual—and a course in charm', *T.E.S.* 28 June 1974). The real answer, of course, lies in an attempt to build a genuinely liberal curriculum on what we know concerning the potential of the low-achievers—concrete but essentially structured. I have attempted to describe such a curriculum (which totally avoids the trivialization of 'courses in charm') in the *T.E.S.* 9 and 15 March 1971, reprinted in *The Curriculum*, ed. R. Hooper. It is, I think, important that we accept that a different curriculum is necessary for sections of our school population; it is equally important that the 'needs' of the low-achievers should not be allowed to dilute the curriculum derived from our 'high' culture.

modern artistic culture, for instance, can be explained in terms of the personal impoverishment implied in theories which are either excessively personal or excessively social in their outlook. In art, action painting and Soviet realism both display a characteristic impoverishment, one through excessive idiosyncrasy, one through excessive conventionality. The schools currently reflect an analogous impoverishment as a result of the impact of progressivism —which is, after all, only the pedagogic manifestation of a general cultural debilitation. The concern for 'nature'—in its several significances—or the collectivity in education are merely particular instances of a general movement towards reductionism and homogenization which constitute the present threat to the future of European culture in a mass age. What has taken place is a shift in man's metaphysical image of himself—from a self that has to be made, to a self that simply has to be expressed. Rousseau's assertion of the importance of childhood as a state in its own right rather than as a potential for actualization marks—paradoxically —a diminution in childhood itself.

Comprehensive Mythology

FRED NAYLOR

In an article in *The Times* (11 October 1974), I welcomed the fact that Mr Prentice had shown himself the first Labour Minister to express concern for educational standards by attempting to produce evidence that secondary organization along comprehensive lines was not, through its intimate involvement with doctrinaire egalitarianism, having a levelling-down effect, as its detractors asserted. Mr Prentice's so-called evidence was in fact shown to be irrelevant to any comparison between the comprehensive and tripartite systems.

He had simply pointed to a 28% increase in 'A' level passes in the secondary system between 1965 and 1972. By failing to examine how this rate of increase compared with what it might have been in the absence of comprehensivization, and whether it was greater in the comprehensive sector than elsewhere during this period of widespread growth, he had fallen into the *post hoc ergo propter hoc* trap. If Mr Prentice, with all the resources at his disposal, could not produce anything better than this, it must be presumed that his case is indeed threadbare. In point of fact his office did have more relevant information, which showed that the expected increase of 40% in the number of school-leavers with two or more 'A' level passes, between 1965 and 1972, had turned out in practice to be only 23%. But this presumably was not known by Mr Prentice.

I went on to argue that Mr Prentice and his predecessors had ignored evidence which was available through two national surveys. The latest (*A Critical Appraisal of Comprehensive Education*, 1972, by the National Foundation for Educational Research in England and Wales), which was commissioned by Mr Anthony Crosland, showed that only one of the 11 fully developed comprehensive schools examined came at or above the national average in respect of the proportion of pupils gaining certificates with two or more 'A' level passes. The other— an earlier N.F.E.R. study (*Achievement in Mathematics*, 1967)—showed that tripartite schools, suitably weighted, were superior to comprehensive schools in the mathematical attainments of their 13, 14 and 15 year olds, and their 'O' level candidates and 'A' level candidates; significantly so for 15 year olds and 'O' level candidates. Astonishingly, the authors, in testing the mathematical achievement of 'A' level mathematicians, were content to point to a relatively small difference in mean score (38.41 to 31.70 in favour of tripartite schools) and failed to draw attention to the fact that the number of pupils who had become 'A' level mathematicians in comprehensive schools was little more than a third of what it was in both grammar and technical schools. The 18 comprehensive schools in the representative sample produced only 83 'A' level mathematicians, whereas the 34 grammar schools had 458 and the eight technical schools had 92.

I also suggested that Mr Prentice's determination to push on with national comprehensivization and to eliminate all alternatives before satisfactory evidence on standards could be obtained would remove any reasonable doubt that the movement was an ideological one, undertaken with the aim of indoctrinating pupils into a pre-selected value system.

The invitation to Mr Prentice to debate the issue on the facts available remains unanswered, and the charge that there is no evidence to suggest that fully developed comprehensive schools—staffed by enthusiasts, be it noted—are capable of matching up even to the mediocrity of the national average has not been refuted.

The nature of the ideology underlying the movement is not difficult to discern. Comprehensive schooling no longer stands for the preservation of the grammar school tradition with the elimination of selection. Doctrinaire egalitarians find the recognition of individual differences through the provision of special courses within a school just as repulsive as the provision of special schools themselves. Ideologically the comprehensive school represents the socialist society in miniature. Just as the doctor, dustman, retired admiral and cabin boy in this society— costing the same to feed, clothe and house decently— would reside in the same street of near-identical houses, so the future doctor, dustman, admiral and cabin boy must be taught together in the same mixed-ability classes, both in the primary and secondary schools, and eventually in the universities too.

We should not be shocked or angry that such an ideology is espoused, or that its proponents wish it to be the basis of their children's education. What should anger us is their attempt to impose this ideology universally, and to ignore or distort the evidence of its real effects when it is put into practice. The attempt to build an immediate practical system around such a remote Utopian ideal is absurd. If it is not halted we can look forward to the collapse not only of our educational system, but of our society as well.

The almost limitless capacity of the Utopians for self-deception is well known; and it would be profitless to inquire why comprehensivists have become convinced—against all the evidence—that comprehensive schools are more successful than the tripartite schools in raising achievement and creating more opportunities, developing a sense of responsibility and fostering good manners—all qualities that most parents would reasonably expect from a good education. It is, however, of immense interest to know why the myth-makers have been able to secure attention and why large sections of the public appear to have allowed themselves to be taken in; coming to believe propositions that are demonstrably untrue and allowing the Utopians a field-day. If we can understand how this came about we might be able to avoid being so gullible in the future.

It might help us to answer this question if we remind ourselves that the myths surrounding our own educational system are matched by myths we entertain about education in other countries. One of the most persistent of these is that the U.S.A. has a comprehensive education system, with selection discredited, and that in pursuing national comprehensivization we are merely following a path that has been well and successfully trodden in the States.

My realization that this was folklore first came with a personal visit to Lowell High School in San Francisco—a public senior high school which had 500 students with I.Q.s of 140 or more in its enrolment of 2,500. It is an academic high school specializing entirely in college preparation. Competition to get in is very keen, and admission is based on previous achievement in junior high.

Selective schools are not of course universal in the U.S.A. They comprise, however, some of the most prestigious and important schools in the country. Apart from San Francisco they are found in Boston, Philadelphia and New York. All these are public schools (i.e. maintained, in our sense). In addition there are numerous private and parochial schools which are predominantly academic, i.e. have college preparation courses only. These nearly all charge fees, but some—like Lick-Wilmerding in San Francisco—are open to those who cannot afford to pay. As in the public sector competition to get into these academic schools is keen and selection occurs. Also in the public sector are special vocational schools, existing alongside the comprehensive and academic high schools. The New York City system—by far the most selective—deserves special attention.

The New York selective system is based on Stuyvesant High School, the Bronx High School for Science and the Brooklyn Technical High School. Stuyvesant is one of the most remarkable schools in the States. So successful is this school, and so concerned is it with bringing out the best in each of its pupils, that almost certainly if it had been situated in England it would long ago have been placed at the top of the list for liquidation by our egalitarians.

Situated just off Second Avenue, Stuyvesant is a special science senior high school and takes in boys of every race, creed and social class from all the five boroughs of the city. It provides specialized training for the intellectually gifted of the city, regardless of background. The school's claim to excellence seems to be amply borne out by the statistics it quotes—the greatest number of Ph.D. degrees in mathematics and science awarded nationally, and the winning of 2,500,000 dollars annually by its students, in college scholarships.

Founded in 1904 the school met with immediate success and pupils began flocking to its doors. Its reaction was to go over to the double-shift system (1920), and for a spell the principal even experimented with triple sessions. The City was fortunate in having administrators who reacted to success by creating new schools on the same model. Thus the Bronx High School for Science was eventually set up to parallel the Stuyvesant programme, and today admission to each is controlled by a common system of testing.

This is not to argue that the comprehensive ideal is not strong in America. The majority of its schools do provide a range of courses, and lip-service is generally paid to the common school. The results are best with good neighbourhood schools—where the comprehensive principle is least in evidence. But growing dissatisfaction with the effect of egalitarian policies on quality and the progress of the able pupil has been expressed. In 1955 the St Louis Public Schools found it necessary to introduce a special programme for superior pupils. These are identified by methods similar to those employed in our 11+ tests, but applied at 9+ instead. Pupils with I.Q.s of 125 or more, with matching performances in standardized tests in reading, language and arithmetic, are entitled to a special programme of work, with specially selected teachers, leading to accelerated progress through the school. There are similar Gifted Children programmes throughout the junior high schools in many states of the U.S.A. The national Advanced Placement Programme for senior pupils was also launched in 1955 in the belief that 'it is better for these students . . . to wallow in a few difficulties than to slumber in indifference'.

The broadly based and prestigious Science Advisory Committee of President Eisenhower in its statement 'Education for an Age of Science', 1959, also had some fierce things to say about the levelling that was occurring in American education. Thus—'we occasionally act as though we feared the word "excellent", especially as applied to mental achievement; as though we felt that there was something strange about the "straight A" student'. It went on to deprecate the view that seemed to require all Americans to be equally competent in intellectual matters and pass together from grade to grade in school, and the notion insinuated into the classroom that all must graduate with the class, lest maladjustment or drop-out ensue. 'Democracy does not require that everyone go to college. By accepting such a shibboleth we can only debase the significance of a college degree.'

There is evidence that the American difficulties are getting worse, not better. Good neighbourhood schools are threatened by community politics, and elsewhere the schools are in disarray with the dilution of academic standards and the growing failure of the teachers to establish any kind of authority. Each school district staggers from crisis to crisis, and teachers have an overwhelming impression that nobody has any time for basic educational issues.

The existence of academic high schools in the private sector does not seem to be under attack at all—thanks to the American tradition of respecting the rights of the individual. Not surprisingly the public academic high schools have been the target of left-wing attack, but their right to exist has been upheld by the Federal Court (Lowell suit 1972 and 1974). It is presumably the openness of American society that guarantees the coexistence of educational philosophies such as that of Stuyvesant—capacity for setting standards, taking legitimate pride in achievement, and honouring those who contribute to the realization of the school's aims—alongside comprehensivism. Possibly, too, there is a realization that the academic high schools are oases in the great egalitarian desert.

Any suspicions that my surprise at these discoveries was due to lack of assiduity in keeping myself informed were dispelled when I found that they were equally surprising to those colleagues—including some who could be expected to be amongst the best informed in this country—with whom

I later discussed my experiences. This ignorance of the American scene must regrettably be attributed in the main to our biased literature.

There is possibly a clue here to account for our own myths. A biased literature and a public lulled into a state of uncritical acceptance of anything put before it—the twin requirements of a mythology—are both manifestations of the 'progressive syndrome', with which we have become increasingly afflicted. We have gradually come to accept, almost without question, the philosophical notion that each state of society is, by some law of nature, an advance on that which preceded it. The implication of such a notion is that if we wish to chart the course for the future we need only look back at recent developments, discern the trend and extrapolate into the future. Such a method, discounting wisdom, regard for objective evidence and principle alike, has spawned a new breed of educationists—the trend-discerners and the trend-setters, whose chief qualifications are a nose for sniffing out exciting novelties and an instinct for spotting likely bandwagons the moment they get under way.

Another factor contributing to the uncritical adoption of comprehensivization has been the behaviour of our politicians. Left-wingers have been consistent in their advocacy of their ideology, even if unwilling to face the fact that the application of their policies has not always led in the direction expected. Politicians of other persuasions have been slow to perceive that the changes have had an ideological basis. Possessing the means to contract out of the state system for the education of their own children, they have until recently been able to take a detached view of state education and concentrate exclusively on vote-winning policies. They thus found themselves committed to placating a small but vocal section of middle-class parents who were apprehensive of their children being excluded from grammar schools when merit became the sole test of entry. Again, support of a system which seemed, on a superficial analysis, to be doing an injustice to four-fifths of the population could hardly be a popular vote-catcher. On top of this many of the same politicians could not resist backing a new movement which seemed to be catching on, and which comprehensive mythology had succeeded in making appear attractive. Not for nothing did the Conservative Minister, when confronted with the public anxiety about what was going on in education, retort: 'And yet the pace of structural change is as fast now as it was under Labour.'

The Equality Merchants: some lessons from abroad

One of the most important, and controversial, areas in education is that centring on the notion of equality. Views on this will stem from basic beliefs about human nature, and are bound to reflect differing ideologies. It is much too sensitive an area for superficiality, and it is therefore disturbing to find the progressive syndrome operating here too. For example, the recent history of our country, as of others, reveals a well-defined trend towards greater equality of opportunity, and towards a greater equality for citizens before the law. It is tempting for the progressive to argue from this that the pursuit of equality more widely— and particularly the substitution of the goal of equality of educational opportunity by that of equality itself—will put him on the side of the angels.

The doctrine that *all* inequalities are to be condemned is both simple and emotionally appealing. It calls only for sloganizing and posturing, and dispenses with the need for serious thought. The fanatical egalitarian need not do anything that is difficult or inconvenient. He can be content to express his moral indignation at any and every inequality, and blame others for the ills. Thus the enthusiastic comprehensivist has on many occasions bought what advantages are to be gained from the private sector for his own children's education, putting the blame on an unequal society and consoling himself with the thought that everything will come right with legislation. He ignores the fact that the strength of a society lies in the character of its individual members, and that where this is lacking the kind of legislation that would be needed to establish his Utopia would be so Draconian as to destroy it at the very moment of its inception.

The fanatical egalitarian slips easily into a simplistic all-or-none approach. Not all parents are given a choice of education for their children in the state system. Therefore none should have a choice. Not all parents are fortunate enough to be able to contract out of the state system of education if they find it unsatisfactory. Therefore none should. The danger of this approach is the way it can lead to dramatic shifts, and even U-turns, by educational policy makers. This is nowhere better illustrated than in the egalitarian influence on public examinations in England. There are only two possible stances on examinations for the egalitarian—examinations for all or examinations for none. Clearly the latter is preferable, since it is a characteristic of examinations to reveal uncomfortable individual differences. But if attempts to abolish examinations have to be abandoned, then examinations for all becomes the new goal. There has been no sadder sight in recent English education than that which followed the introduction of the Certificate of Secondary Education in 1965, when 'abolitionists' almost overnight became the champions for the extension of examining down to the 100th pupil percentile.

But the greatest threat posed by egalitarianism is its ultimate effect on freedom. Those who talk of equality in the schools *and* of giving pupils programmes suited to their needs are talking dangerous nonsense. It seems, however, that one can adduce weighty philosophical arguments to show that liberty and equality are incompatible and yet fail to carry conviction. Perhaps this is because it is not sufficiently emphasized that the loss of liberty entails glaring injustices to individuals. A concrete example might serve where dialectic fails.

When the educational principles on which Lowell High School was run were challenged in the U.S. Federal Court the charges of discrimination by race and class were dismissed, but that of discrimination by sex was upheld. The condition complained of was that around 45% of the school's pupils were boys, whereas around 55% were girls. Those attuned to sex-lib situations here would no doubt be quick to extend their sympathy to the boys as obvious victims of sex discrimination. But wait. It turns out that Lowell was being indicted for showing favouritism to boys not girls! This seeming paradox is explained by the fact that if admission to the school had been decided entirely on merit over 60% of the pupils would have been girls. Egalitarians had jibbed at this. Although they had not been successful in securing a balance of the sexes in the school, they had given a big push in this direction by establishing a higher admission grade for girls than for boys. In following egalitarian policies the school had unjustly discriminated against many individual girls, as the court had no difficulty in establishing.

This example should serve as a warning to those tempted to try to engineer the intake into any institution, or onto any course, on the basis of the proportions of certain categories in the total population—whether these be founded on sex, class or race. If it can be shown that any person of merit has thereby been excluded there is an open-and-shut case that discrimination has been practised.

The most striking feature of many of our present left-wing proposals for equality in education is that they go very much further than it has been found possible to go in countries that might be considered of like mind. Thus in Sweden—where lip-service is paid both to equality and the right of every child to a free choice of course—potential entrants to the gymnasium (and hence to university) are virtually determined towards the end of Grade 6, i.e. at the age of 13.[1] Furthermore the percentage of the age group to be admitted to the gymnasium has been fixed by Parliamentary decision at a maximum of 30%. Comprehensive education is supposed to operate up to the age of 16, but in practice selection starts at the age of 13. The difference between what is supposed to happen and what really does happen seems to be a general characteristic of the Swedish educational system.

But it is a study of the U.S.S.R. that is most rewarding in a critical appraisal of myths and an examination of the extent to which it is safe to push egalitarian policies. George Bernard Shaw in his attack on the Equality Merchants [2] pointed out that the Government of the U.S.S.R. started with the intention of giving all workers an equal share of the national income that their labour was producing, but found that they were not producing enough to give each of them more than the pittance earned by the cheapest labour under Tsardom. Equality of income had therefore to be dropped until the national dividend could be raised to the professional level. Although, declared Shaw, it was easy for a democratic statesman to jump to the conclusion that, as we all cost the same to feed, clothe and house decently no matter how our abilities vary, the simple solution is to give us all the same share of the national income, this would bring him up against the fact that it costs more to produce an admiral than a cabin boy, though their needs as human beings are the same. As Shaw concluded, if we reduce them to a common denominator we shall get a superfluity of cabin boys and no admirals. The situation is still basically unchanged in the U.S.S.R. after over half a century of tough grappling with the problem.

As in its approach to economics, so in education, Russia —after an initial period of experimentation (1917–31) with ideas that bear a striking resemblance to the most radical of our present ideas, and which ended in disaster as the teacher's authority in the schools became nil—with characteristic realism adapted its policies to the practicalities of the situation. The most important change concerned its attitude towards competition. At first this was identical with the one widely prevalent in influential quarters in England today. But it soon found that it could not do without competition. It did not take it long to discern a difference between unhealthy and healthy competition. The unhealthy kind was based on the competition found in nature, where the life of one creature was secured only at the cost of the death of its rivals: the successful used the bodies of their competitors to climb to the top. Healthy competition, or socialist competition—so important that the Russian language was called upon to furnish a special word (*sotssorevnovaniye*) to describe it— had, on the other hand, the aim of bringing out the best in each individual for the good of society. And this did not only apply to team competition—the award of the red challenge banner to the most productive work teams—but also included awards for meritorious individual effort, such as gold medals for top students and passes to holiday homes for outstanding workers fulfilling or exceeding their production targets.

If there is one single thing that would most help English education at present it would be a careful rethinking of our

attitude to competition, pondering the significance of socialist competition in Russia.

The matching of children to courses in the U.S.S.R. could not of course be done by means of tests which measure potential. Although Lysenko never went as far as denying the function of genes in shaping the development of individuals, it has been a constant theme of Soviet biology that the genes could always be shaken up and made to dance to the tune of the operator, be he agronomist or educator. The emphasis on the effects of the environment at the expense of heredity was not something to be decided solely on the evidence. It was the only view consistent with the Marxist faith.

Although Soviet children are allocated to school classes initially on the assumption that they are all alike, promotion from class to class is strictly by merit, and 'repeating' is therefore a prominent feature of Soviet schooling. The figures given by Korol [3] in 1955 showed that between 10% and 30%, depending on the grade, were 'repeaters' at any one time. Grant,[4] in 1966, placed the general figure a good deal higher than the 4% officially claimed for Leningrad, and quoted a remark by Kruschev that 20% of the pupils repeated so often that they never completed the seven-year course. Hearnden [5] (1973) puts the proportion of grade-repeaters for the country as a whole at about 20%, a figure supported by information I have received in recent conversations with Soviet teachers. The system is not selective at entry, but vertical selection operates throughout. There is no sentimental egalitarianism here, as the competitive pressures, backed up by a strong public feeling, create an urge to work for success. Russian realism again offsets the worst effects of doctrinaire egalitarianism.

In more recent years special schools for exceptionally gifted pupils have been appearing. The special boarding schools for gifted mathematicians are the best known, but day schools specializing in mathematics and physics have been established in the large cities. They reflect a widespread feeling that the system still does not do enough for the able Soviet youth.

A look ahead

What needs to be done in view of the confusion, uncertainty and mystification that surround education at the present time? The first thing to recognize is that we are, for good or ill, an open society. Officially we may have an established Church, and a commitment to Christian worship and non-denominational religious instruction in our schools. But the reality is that, though this is adhered to strictly in some schools, it is only followed with great difficulty in many, and is a sham in others. People are choosing to go their own ways. Though it may be true that society needs a greater moral consensus than exists today, if it is to hold together, any attempt at a central imposition of an ideology to fill the existing moral vacuum would not only be wrong, but could also prove disastrous with the country in its present mood. The devolution movements reflect the desire of individuals, and groups of individuals, to gain greater control over the decisions which affect their life— including the education of their children.

The state of our education today is uncannily like that of American education when it began to go sour. Writing in *The Way out of Educational Confusion* in 1931, John Dewey described it thus:

There is nothing accepted as axiomatic, nothing beyond the possibility of questioning, and few things that are not actually attacked. Conservatives who urge return to

[1] A. G. Hearnden, *Preparation, Assessment and Selection for University*. Schools Council/Oxford University Department of Educational Studies, 1973.
[2] G. B. Shaw, 'Everybody's Political What's What'. *Essay on Equality*, 1944.

[3] A. Korol, *Soviet Professional Manpower*. National Science Foundation, Washington D.C., 1955.
[4] Nigel Grant, *Soviet Education*. 1964, Penguin 1970.
[5] Hearnden, op. cit.

former standards and practices and radicals who criticize present conditions agree at least on one point: neither party is satisfied with things as they are. . . . As far as uncertainty about standards, purposes, tendencies and methods leads to discussion, there is something healthy about it. Doubt and questioning, no matter how far they go, are not in themselves an occasion for pessimism. But mere confusion is not a good thing. There is a confusion due to the smoke of battle obscuring the scene from the onlooker; and there is a different confusion due to combatants losing sight of what they are doing and where they are going, a chaos of uncoordinated movements and actions.

If we are prepared to accept that we are an open society there must be provision for appropriate debate, of a kind more honest than we have so far been used to. It must be widely understood that the enemies of education are not those who criticize new ideas or question progressive shibboleths. They are those who, for whatever reason, uncritically adopt or hold any view, of whatever shade or complexion, without being able to justify or defend it. And if, after honest debate, we find ourselves really fundamentally opposed on basic aims, or ideologies, there is really no alternative—if we wish to remain a democracy—to allowing free expression in our educational system for them all. It is more than likely that in this new climate we would find that our differences were concerned with means, rather than ends, to a greater extent than we had imagined. Such differences are capable of being settled by appeal to experience, obtained through carefully controlled experiments or accruing from the variety there would be under such an open system.

We could very largely free ourselves from our myths and be in a position to allow parents to have an informed say in what should be provided. We could look forward to progress in settling our most important and thorniest educational problem—the limits that need to be set on the pursuit of equality. If this could be done—and it is admittedly a very tall order—we would be on the way to establishing the greater consensus that must be our ultimate goal if the democratic fabric of our society is to be preserved.

Why Comprehensives Fail

G. KENNETH GREEN

In 1956 when I moved to teach in a newly opened, purpose-built comprehensive school, we were all, I believe, inspired and informed by the need to establish real equality of opportunity in education. Most of us saw the lack of this as an area of concern which was not being satisfied by the tripartite system, because we were unable to ignore the increasing evidence of high academic and creative potential in the secondary modern and technical schools. We believed that the comprehensive school could go some way to help to avoid the creation of a divided society; not that we could by a different pattern of organization create the ideal of Christian brotherliness, but we expected that, at least, a real and mutual appreciation between the different strata of the social system might result. In academic and social terms we hoped that the traditions of excellence, integrity, altruism, and sense of service established by the grammar schools could inform the day-by-day school life of all children, as we thought these ideals were at the very root of quality in education.

This was not to say that the secondary modern and technical schools were not doing excellent work within their terms of reference, but, like the grammar schools, they had limitations in terms of staffing, equipment and the flexible breadth of courses offered. The process of selection at 11+ was suspect and irrevocable in too many cases, and we were interested in offering quality and achievement for all children. In those halcyon and somewhat innocent days, we were guided by educational considerations; schools were seen, as they should still be, as institutions of learning and discipline in the very widest sense of that much abused word; and we regarded them as guardian-transmitters of all that was good from the past into the present. The idea of 'social engineering' had not begun to spread its insidious poison, and, in my own discipline, we still taught English, not a nasty hybrid of civics and sociology. We believed, finally, that to be labelled 'comprehensive' a school should certainly cater for the whole range of academic ability and that its intake should have that range of ability and be *in balance*. Since then there have been increasingly persistent and misguided attempts not only to throw out the baby with the bath water, but also to destroy the bath itself. We have suffered an unthinking rush into change not only in terms of organizational pattern, but also in curriculum matters, and have developed a guilt complex about any form of stability.

Equality of opportunity—a realizable and common-sense objective—has over the past decade been replaced by the objective of *equality*, at the same time a political and biological absurdity. The reorganized school system has been seen as a way of achieving this aim, with disastrous effects on curricula, and standards of achievement in every respect. Is it now acceptable that the overall academic achievement in Manchester schools as measured by the C.S.E. and by G.C.E. 'O' and 'A' levels should be much lower in the reorganized situation? All men should be equal in the eyes of the law and are so in the eyes of God, but any schoolmaster of even limited experience will tell you that the great joy of his work lies in the differences— academic, social, creative, emotional—between children. It is right that compensatory programmes should be implemented and used to redress social deprivation, but we make a grave mistake, as many amateur educationists have done, if we imagine that any system of programmes will eliminate intrinsic natural differences between children—

some children are better at some activities than others. This is an inescapable fact:

> To be given equality of opportunity is the right of every child: to expect equal capacity to make use of this opportunity runs counter to common sense and experience. In fact, it has harmful consequences because such expectation is bound to engender a sense of failure. (M. Kellmer Pringle, *Able Misfits*.)

The comprehensive school, like any school, should recognize this fact and work with it, ensuring that the uniqueness of the individual is preserved as far as is possible, and ensuring that all children are made to feel that justice is being done to them and everyone else, and that they are valued for what they are and for what they have to offer, whatever it be. Regrettably, comprehensive schools, because many of them have no recognizable academic goal, have a distorted picture of enrichment/compensatory programmes and much of our education over the past decade has been steered away from the able towards the average and less than average. We are, and have been, exchanging excellence for mediocrity and in the process are beginning to create a pool of frustration and deprivation among able children:

> In spite of popular prejudice there is, or there should be, no insuperable conflict between equality as a principle of justice and inequality as a fact of genetics. In education equal opportunity means equal opportunity to make the most of differences that are innate. The ideal is a free and fair chance to each individual not to rise to the same rank in life as everyone else, but to develop the peculiar gifts and virtues with which he is endowed—high ability if he possesses it, if not, whatever qualities of body, mind and character are latent within him. (Sir Cyril Burt, 1962.)

The supporters of the notion of equality have been reinforced by a persistent, vociferous anti-intellectual faction most evident in comprehensive schools, some universities and among politically motivated educationists. 'Academic', 'intellectual', have become almost pejorative terms; 'formal', 'traditional', words of abuse; 'progressive', 'forward-looking', words of divine revelation. Teachers as a group have been brainwashed into thinking that there must be something wrong with them if they are interested in the needs of the able, of preserving standards of learning and attainment, of believing that things were not always badly done thirty years ago. However, the writing is on the wall for all to see; the flight from the reorganized, maintained sector has not only begun, it is becoming a flood. Instead of introducing doctrinal legislation in a panic-stricken way, our administrators need to examine very closely the reasons which are impelling so many parents to choose to spend quite considerable sums of money, in addition to their taxes, to send their children to schools out of the maintained system. The root causes are a profound disquiet about academic and social standards; about learning and discipline; about culture and anarchy. There is evidence in London and elsewhere of increasing consumer resistance to 'progressive', 'do-your-own-thing' secondary schools, be they never so well endowed with buildings and equipment. Parents are preferring neighbouring schools where the physical conditions are perhaps less prepossessing but where the atmosphere is one of discipline and where learning takes place. It is a sad fact that many parents have to endure for their children 'educational' practices of which they do not approve, being fobbed off with comments about 'learning readiness', 'self-awareness', 'self-development' as substitutes for the fundamental securities of teaching and learning, Parents in this situation, who can afford to, choose the private school.

To cut off the independent sector in a fit of pique with pious protestations about 'privilege' is really to ignore the disease which is making the independent school seem more desirable as a *school* than so many in the comprehensive, maintained sector.

Many schools labelled 'comprehensive' are nothing of the sort, first and foremost because they have no academic top and, as a direct consequence of this, have a level of academic aspiration and attainment which can only be mediocre. It is no answer for the unthinking proponents of 'reorganization' to cry that all will be well if all the grammar schools, direct grant and independent schools are abolished and the displaced children sucked into the new system. The only results of wholesale dismemberment will be, as they have been in many areas, that a system of proven value will be removed and nothing of equal value will be put in its place, and the children so displaced will suffer from being offered an education which is much less than they and their parents, in natural and educational justice, have a right to expect. Many reorganized schools are multi-site, and I know from my own experience that although it is possible to keep such institutions running efficiently in terms of organization and administration their educational efficiency is suspect because of the additional demands on use of time, and the expenditure of nervous energy from staff and children moving from one building to another, very often some distance apart. In addition, the disposition of the accommodation, almost as much as the academic intake, dictates what can be offered in the curriculum to the children.

One of the major factors in the indiscipline and truancy from large schools is the fact that they are large agglomerations of children of average and less than average abilities. Many of these children lack motivation and provide almost insuperable problems of backwardness/retardation, of maladjustment and anti-social behaviour. One of the great strengths of the secondary modern school was that its difficult children were well known to the staff, and the numbers were small enough to be controlled and reasonably effectively dealt with. It was much easier with smaller numbers to check attendance at school or lesson. One of the greatest weaknesses of many 'comprehensives' is that they offer 'academic' fare to children not capable of handling it. Further exacerbation of these difficulties lies in the fact that it is expected of schools to wear 'sack-cloth and ashes' and accept that truancy is their fault; but the guilt lies fairly and squarely with factions in the politics of education who encourage abdication of responsibility, condone anti-social acts and demand liberal—but insecure in emotional terms—schools. Free schools and truant centres are the latest gimmicks of self-deception: they provide further excuses for lack of co-operation and responsibility from parents and public, and further erode the authority and position of schools and teachers. Instead of the ideas of community living and social behaviour informing the whole atmosphere of the school, and the children developing, as it were, outwards to the wider community from that point, they are now offered courses in sociology and social education, a paste-board imitation of the real experience.

Because of the materialistic, commercial and emotional pressures exerted by the media and modern life generally, there is a greater need than ever for structure, stability and calm in schools. There is an obvious bewilderment in children because there is no 'authority' on which they can rely, because there is no invisible pattern of restriction and expectation against which they can test themselves as people and by which they can be supported when this is needed. It is quite possible for an institution informally organized, accepting all standards and therefore offering none, to be so large and amorphous as to engender insecurity, additional instability and panic. I believe that children instinctively expect a school to offer an attitude and philosophy—whether they ultimately accept or reject these does not matter. They expect teachers to be adults not 'mates'; they expect to be given the opportunity to learn; they expect to have the fullest opportunities to obtain qualifications because they live in the real world and so do their parents. Parents have firm ideas about what they want for their children, and those who have deserted, and are deserting, the maintained sector for the independent, have done so because they know what they want and where they can get it. These are the positively motivated parents and pupils which the maintained sector needs as its leavening.

There has been an increasingly active movement against the size of comprehensive schools—one can cite the London area as an example—from parents who want a disciplined framework for their children in which learning can take place. There is unquestionably a point at which numbers in a school begin to be counter-productive, and the advantages that can be obtained from the wide variety of staff qualifications and interests begin to be first inhibited, and then nullified by the administrative, supervisory, and communication problems involved. The point at which this breakdown occurs in the 'size spectrum' differs according to the academic standards and motivation of the institution, but in the case of most of the comprehensive schools we have created, it is well below 1,000 pupils. By reducing numbers of pupils in a school by means of a three- or four-tier system, a further set of problems has been substituted concerning continuity of teaching from first to middle school; the introduction of specialisms such as science, French, Latin, and, again, continuity on transfer to a high school. One can speculate, too, on the effect the 'stop and start' nature of this kind of reorganization will have on children's academic and social progress.

The complex pattern of British education is being further complicated by the appearance of different patterns of educational provision at secondary level in different areas. Some L.E.A.s have opted for the 11–18 school; some for the middle school 8–12 or 9–13, a high school 12/13–16 and a sixth-form college, some for a high school 12/13–18. We live in a mobile society, and the difficulties of a child transferring at the secondary stage, even a short distance, from one L.E.A. to another, sometimes pose incredible problems of readjustment in fitting not only into a new pattern of schooling but also into different syllabuses in almost every subject which should form part of the basis of a broadly based liberal education. One could perhaps feel happier about existing patterns of reorganization were it not that many of them have been imposed for political reasons and have been arrived at by L.E.A. administrations on the basis of existing buildings. Too often the criterion has been one by which the building available determined a kind of organization that could be followed—there ensues a desperate search for a philosophy to fit the new organization; precious little, if any, evaluation has been attempted of patterns already in existence and the in-service training offered to teachers to prepare them for the new situation has been minimal. 'Heads and teachers, as professionals, will ensure that it works' seems to have been the rather dubious watchword of many education committees. There has been such incessant and haphazard tinkering with the educational machine—organizational and curricular—over the past decade, that stability for a five-year term, the general span of most children at secondary level, has become an impossibility.

In terms of reorganization, too much has been attempted too fast in a context of threatening imposition from some education committees and, from time to time, from central government. Too little evaluation of what has been done has taken place and we are stumbling along blindly, hopefully, leaving chaos and confusion behind us. We have been too concerned with *systems* as solutions to educational problems, just as we have been too obsessed with 'hardware' as a panacea for curricular ones. We have rushed into a disastrous situation of our own making. The revolutionary ethic will not work in education because it engenders just those things we can least afford as a society—instability, insecurity, mediocrity and, ultimately, repressive conformity. The evolutionary approach is the only way; it is slower yet more certain, and each successive change is built on the foundation of a previously proved one. It recognizes that people need time and preparation to adjust themselves to new patterns and orders so that they can work in calm and security. We need first to re-establish the authority and status of the teacher by complete and unequivocal support of schools from Education Committees, governors and L.E.A.s. One can, over recent years, cite anti-teacher attitudes which have been reported in the national press and which have eroded the status and authority of the profession.

There needs to be a reassessment of the 11–18 schools in many authorities to establish that they are, indeed, viable academic entities. In the case of some schools, there needs to be a reassessment of *function* so that the school can be staffed appropriately and can do a realistic job in terms of the pupils who attend and the area it serves.

All inspector/advisers should spend a great deal more of their time *evaluating realistically* the worth of the reorganized situation. L.E.A.s should take a realistic view of their resources and use them wisely. There is no point in creating problems and uncertainties in large secondary schools by imagining that all shortage specialist subjects, such as craft and business studies, are going to be covered. It is far better to use staff in positive concentrations where a real job can be done, rather than spreading them so thinly that nobody benefits. It would be no bad thing either if a voluntary restriction of over-complex options in large secondary schools were encouraged. Such proliferations which have burgeoned in many comprehensives are expensive of staff and of doubtful educational value to many pupils. Any saving, in these terms, at secondary level could be used to improve ratios in infant and junior schools where the vital work of social training is done, and literacy and numeracy are acquired.

The Developing Case for the Educational Voucher

RHODES BOYSON

If all primary and secondary schools were working successfully then there would be no need to suggest radical alternatives. Widespread dissatisfaction with progressive primary schools and concern about falling standards of discipline and academic achievement in secondary, particularly comprehensive schools, must force educationalists and administrators to look for some means of improvement. Minimum national standards, as a further expansion of monitoring by examinations, is one method. The other method is to put the parent (and older pupils) as consumers in charge of schools.

It could be argued that the introduction of state-controlled and provided education from 1870 onwards was all a mistake. In his first draft of the 1870 Education Bill, W. E. Forster argued that his objective was to 'fill the gaps' in private education. It was certainly not the intention of the Victorians to destroy parental choice and involvement. If the 1870 Act had simply provided the poor with a 'ticket' or voucher to buy education then the rapidly expanding private schools would have quickly met all the remaining demand.

It is in the U.S.A. that the voucher—a means of enabling the parent to buy education in a market—has been tried. This is not surprising since genuine public participation is supported more in America than in Britain. As early as 1790 Tom Paine, author of *The Rights of Man*, worked out in Virginia a method whereby poor families could receive an annual grant of £4 for each child under the age of 14, which they had to spend on the education of their children.

Support for the educational voucher in the U.S.A. has often come from the left, horrified by the collapse of city ghetto schools. The left in Britain generally prefers to ignore the problems of city ghetto schools and pretends that more money, a further lowering in the pupil-teacher ratio and more equipment will solve all problems.

In Alum Rock, in California, some 13 public (state) schools, ten primary and three middle schools (10–14 years), began a voucher experiment in 1972. There were a variety of courses in each school—22 in all—so that parents could choose not only between schools but between specific courses within schools. The area would be called 'deprived' in the United Kingdom, with 50% Mexican-American, 10% black and 5% Asian.

The voucher is worth $780 for primary school children and $1,050 for middle school children, which represents the average cost of education in the area. Half the children—those coming from low-income families—receive an additional compensatory voucher of $275. This supplement was introduced in an attempt to make the poorest children, whom no school wanted, more valuable so that all schools competed for them and prepared special programmes to attract their support. This has proved much more successful in raising the levels of achievement of children from poor families than any of the schemes of reverse discrimination introduced in Britain.

In the first year (1972–3) when 3,800 children took part, only 130 pupils moved to schools different from the neighbourhood schools to which they would have been directed, but the fact that pupils could and did move had its effect on all schools which had to look to their standards and to their achievements.

In 1973–4 when 9,000 children took part, it was significant that 40% of parents with two or more children chose different courses for their different children, thereby proving that they did understand their children's individual differences of temperament and ability at least as well as did local bureaucrats.

It is interesting that the variety of courses offered within the schools has brought about a form of optional 'tracking' or streaming whereby pupils themselves, with the help of their families and their teachers, have chosen their courses to suit their intellectual abilities and technical aptitudes. Such tracking, being chosen by pupils themselves to maximize their achievements, has brought none of the resentment occasionally arising from streaming in British schools.

Under this Alum Rock programme the involvement of parents has broken all records, the attendance of the pupils has improved and the teaching staff, at first hostile and suspicious, has been won round by the keener interest of parents and pupils despite the greater demands made upon them.

In Alum Rock all schools must provide a full education for the voucher. In September 1974 another voucher experiment started in La Rochelle in New Hampshire, embracing both 'public' and non-sectarian private schools, with parents being allowed to add their own money to supplement the voucher where private schools charge more.

The state assembly of Connecticut has passed special legislation to permit a full voucher experiment in the state. Three more school districts in Milwaukee (Wisconsin), Dayton (Ohio) and Rochester (New York) are beginning inquiries into the feasibility of regulated voucher schemes.

The time would seem ripe for the establishment of at least two full voucher experiments in Britain where local education authorities were anxious to co-operate, as some have already indicated. A non-transferable voucher could be issued for each pupil and the parent would be able to pay it into the school of his choice, either state or private. The school would in turn exchange the vouchers for cash from the state or the local education authority at a value equal to the average cost of state education in that area for the relevant age group. Popular schools would continue and expand and unpopular schools would decline and close.

The state would then have guaranteed an education to all its children, the minimum standards of which could be checked by inspection, and the parents would monitor schools according to their aims and achievements. The very fact that schools were dependent on individual parental choice for their continuance would ensure both accountability and variety. Meanwhile the involvement of the parents in choosing a school would ensure a family's close continued contact. This continued contact was what the Plowden Report suggested was, next to the innate ability of the pupil, the most decisive factor in the success of a pupil's schooling.

It is likely that under the voucher the quality of all schooling would rise so much that even the worst school would then be better in absolute quality than the general run of today's schools. Parents would also probably insist on different courses within the monolithic, egalitarian comprehensive schools before they sent their children there.

The later 1970s could be an ideal time to introduce the voucher because the falling birthrate would mean that there would be redundant school buildings in which new independent schools could be opened by teachers, trusts, churches and other voluntary bodies subject to enforcing a minimum requirement on the record and qualifications of the teaching staff. It will be interesting to see which political party will be both wise and radical enough to introduce such an educational voucher as an experiment both in participating democracy and in raising the standards of general schooling.

'To Give an Education'

JACQUES BARZUN

Some months ago the *New York Times* congratulated itself and the nation editorially because high school pupils were now being graduated with a ninth-grade reading ability, instead of an eighth-grade as in previous years. Everybody today is so inured to paradoxes in education that this curious plus-out-of-minus evoked no embarrassment or sardonic humour. The daily fare of educational news that matters is school vandalism, teachers' strikes, and 'innovation'—such as letting corridors become 'study halls', where, lying on their stomachs, boy-and-girl pairs can lay their heads together over their 'module' of 'language arts', at their own pace and free at last of classroom oppression.

In this state of public opinion, anyone who asks why pupils completing secondary school have for years been receiving its diploma though performing like their juniors in the last year of primary, is just simple-minded. The further question: How did we get to such a pass? is antiquarian irrelevance. Yet some people do wonder in private and a few are courageous enough to expostulate in public: 'It is easy to say that more money is needed to solve our present educational system's failures, but to funnel more money through a system that has proven it does not work is to continue to perpetrate a crime . . . on our children and our country.' (Letter to the *New York Times*, 20 July 1974.)

What then is the meaning—if any—of 150 years of American faith and investment in free public education? At first, when the system worked, it fulfilled part of the American Dream which Horace Mann summed up in the slogan: 'Education is the gateway to Equality'. It was the free public school that assimilated the great waves of nineteenth-century immigration and served the self-betterment for which they swept over America. When Mann in the 1830s was persuading the people to tax themselves for a common schooling, the argument was that the one nation founded on the free pursuit of happiness should provide the means to it in the form of the three Rs.

It was assumed that the people would seize and cherish the gift forever—a reasonable expectation considering the pent-up demand and the makeshifts then in use. Artisans, farmers, and factory workers coveted the powers of literacy, and for its sake made sacrifices as touching as the Thames waterboy's answer to Dr Johnson, who had asked him what he would give to know about the Argonauts: 'Sir, I would give what I have.' What has happened to that appetite is the guiding thread through the tangled history of public education since the great legislative acts of the 1870s.

These were not solely benevolent; they were necessitated by industry and democracy. 'We must educate our masters,' said Robert Lowe after the passage of the Reform Bill of 1867. And it was clear that efficient work in factory or office required ever greater numbers of people who could read and write. In two generations a high level of literacy was attained throughout the western world. But soon the critics of the nascent mass culture perceived that the three Rs did not suffice to spread civilization. Matthew Arnold was the best qualified to speak of educational measures and his refrain was: 'Organize your secondary schools.'

In the United States the same programme was the natural extension of equal opportunity; and its product, the free high school of the early 1900s, was a notable achievement. Its first graduates could be called educated men and women, at least those that followed the so-called academic course. It required Latin including the reading of Virgil and two years of a modern foreign language; it offered two other languages, as well as Greek; it carried mathematics through solid geometry and third-year algebra; it taught Shakespeare and Milton and the great novelists, living and dead; and it laid a good grounding in physics (required) plus either chemistry or biology, while giving corresponding attention to American and European history, with some notions of political society under the name of Civics.

All this has gone like a mirage. Indeed, such a curriculum is to be found only in a few unreformed colleges and universities, where the faculty, still able to spell the word 'requirement', is fighting a rearguard action against the pressure to make all courses elective, contemporary—and invertebrate. One may say that the spirit of the progressive school, potent since the 1920s, has at last breached higher education.

Meanwhile, in the elementary grades the corollary spirit of de-schooling has taken firm hold. As the argument runs, 'disadvantaged children'—white or coloured, English-speaking or not—*cannot* be taught by any means, do not *need* to learn school subjects, do not *want* 'bourgeois values', and consequently *should not* be forced to barter their 'native culture' for scholastic nonsense. The appetite of the last century has, it seems, turned to revulsion in the teachers themselves, the hunger in the pupils to vomiting. Let the school confine itself to 'helping' these slum children—help them speak and write 'Black English', sing Mexican or Puerto Rican folksongs, build up their morale

28

with stories of their races' and classes' unjustly neglected past.

The progressive doctrine of need (I want, therefore I need), which is so popular in the negative, finds here its extreme. But it would be wrong to make it the sole cause. One must look beyond the doctrine to its first motives and later uses. For the progressive plan, devised by philosophers and psychologists, soon split into two purposes, one highly intellectual, the other anti-intellectual. The aim of the one was to overcome the faults of schools as such, by giving the children of liberal academics a quasi-tutorial, custom-made self-education. It presupposed high academic ability in teacher and taught.

The other scheme was to find in progressivism the solution to the gravest problem of the free public school—the lack of teachers. Low status and poor reward explain only part of the shortage. The number of born teachers is small; the number of those who can train or be trained to act like teachers is not indefinitely augmentable. Therefore, shift teacher training away from intellect and towards more common gifts—sympathy, patience, tolerance of confusion, amateur psychologizing, improvising plays, playing games, filling scrapbooks, administering tests, guiding visits to aquariums and power plants—the whole battery of devices for evading the hard work of systematically removing ignorance—and you circumvent the permanent obstacles to expanding a school system in scale with a modern population.

Besides natural dearth, changes in society seemingly unrelated to education conspired to undermine the school; for example, the emancipation of women. Up to World War I, the spinster was a prime educational force. Unmarried perhaps because of father worship, she was often well-educated and a born disciplinarian, yet with maternal feelings to express. The wider, freer postwar world was bound to change the style and reduce the supply of women teachers. The new freedom was desirable, but the relaxation of manners which went with the loosening of family bonds, and which weakened authority and hierarchy generally, also worked against effective schooling. For if one thing is inherently hierarchical it is the substance of learning. You cannot study physics before mastering the multiplication table, which is a completely authoritarian document. The reason for its authority can be grasped only by those who have first taken it on faith and learned 'higher' things besides. It was an irony of nomenclature that progressive education should base so many of its 'methods' on the denial of such progression.

Several other facts of our century contributed to the absolute falling off of 'instructional productivity' in Western culture, and hence to the decline and fall of the school as an intellectually formative institution. In the 1930s the desire to make the school the cradle of reform diverted it still more sharply from its simple goal; after World War II a fresh cause was the euphoria of 'innovation'. It is again a paradox of advanced thought that the liberal will to manipulate society through the school unconsciously aped totalitarian practice, and that innovation for its own sake is the dogma of industrialists, whom many school people affect to scorn.

The upshot of all this bad thinking (done, no doubt, under adverse conditions) has been the revolt of the ultimate consumer—the pupil. He dimly knows that he is mistreated and clearly knows that he is bored. He thus has the leisure to pass judgment on his mentors, who are fumbling, quarreling, picketing, and for the most part not teaching. When it is normal to be promoted each year to a higher grade regardless of failure, mutual trust and respect disappear, the *morality* of compulsory schooling no longer holds. Cheating at examinations becomes a pastime, as little blamable as the school heads' periodic reports of falsified marks to obtain various benefits for their schools, teachers, and pupils. The high school diploma which then leads into 'open admission' colleges is the fit certificate of the Big Lie. But once the pretence of honest and orderly conduct is blown, there is nothing illogical about blowing up the school and—why not?—the teacher with it.

Some teachers and some teaching do survive, of course; there is some opposition to the laying waste. When educationists declare that reading will soon be obsolete, thanks to improved television means, the Council for Basic Education deflates the vain imagining—at least for its members. When 'Black English' gains support in high literary circles, Dr Kenneth Clark, the distinguished black psychologist, denounces the pernicious folly. Again, when Mr Blouke Carus, the head of Open Court Books, found that his children in public school were droning their way through the Dick-and-Jane readers, he started a publishing programme to reintroduce style and meaning, and with them the phonic way to learn the alphabet. When expensive but shoddy statistics 'showed' that schools have no effect and the pupil's fate is set by his 'background', Mr George Weber (of the Council) undertook a study proving that five slum schools outdid the national averages in reading ability. And he ascertained the cause: the man or woman principal who knows what a school is for and who energizes his staff to act on that knowledge. So 'school' today need not revert to its etymological sense of 'idleness'. The *New York Times* duly noted this by giving front-page attention to Mr Weber's discovery.

But the question of why defeatism prevails so largely and easily still remains. The answer is that a great collective fear grips all but the stoutest hearts, the Tocquevillean democratic fear—of seeming superior, of exercising authority, of imposing a standard, of causing pain by naming failure, inadequacy, or ignorance. In short, it is the fear of others' envy masquerading as the love of equality. The response of the able school principals to Mr Weber's study is characteristic: they were appalled at the favourable notice of their work; they pretended the achievement was negligible, fortuitous, unintentional. The motive was not modesty but fear—justified in the event when they suffered hostile words and acts from their superiors and their 'equals' alike.

Horace Mann would not recognize this distorted emotion as the logical result of his practical plan. His contemporaries were no less jealous, but they were less crowded and driven, more used to risk and self-reliance. They wanted to equalize men's start in life, not the outcome. It would not have occurred to them, as it lately has to us, that it was possible to *give an education* as one gives the needy a hot meal or a warm coat. Their plain thought was that education should be *offered*, and by the able *acquired*. It is important to add that they did not overvalue academic labels as we do. So much has been said and done to prove the social and economic worth of the badge that it is now deemed indispensable to success and self-respect. That is why in a society striving to be fair-minded it has to be *given*; at which point there is in truth no need of schools, colleges, or universities.

Teachers Speak Out

Experiences in an Open Plan Primary School

The school was opened in April 1971 with about 60 children on roll which rose rapidly to its present total of 290 + 15 E.S.N. children in a purpose-built unit. Of the staff originally appointed only the headmaster and one teacher still remain. The original staff were appointed on a temporary basis and left after the first term. Since then the staff turnover has been very high. A large percentage of teachers appointed were probationers (totally unsuitable to cope in a difficult area) and left after their first year.

The school is built on the edge of a city overspill estate adjacent to the countryside and in a very pleasant position. Most of the families have been moved from old houses in the city where their families had lived close to one another for generations and where a five- or ten-minute bus ride would take them to the city centre. They now find themselves in lovely new houses in the country which they hate, and miles from their relatives. The bus service to the city is regular but takes 45 minutes and is expensive. They don't take to the quiet country life and the whole family is unsettled. What these children need is the stable, disciplined environment of a conventional school building.

The school is virtually a continuous corridor built round the central hall. It is impossible to confine any class because there are no doors. Children can disappear easily and the teacher cannot be expected to keep track of every child. Truancy is a big problem which has been aggravated by the opening of a sweet shop close by the school. We've tried locking all outside doors (which is against fire regulations) but children just get out through the windows or wait till play time and run off then. The assembly hall is used for music and P.E. and also acts as a general thoroughfare. Because of the design of the school any teacher or child needing to go to the head or secretary must go through the hall. In one half-hour choir practice we had 27 different children walk through the hall. This is very irritating and frustrating and rather like teaching in Piccadilly Circus.

The organization and discipline in the school are virtually non-existent and there is no ultimate threat one can make to a disobedient child. Many of our children come from disturbed or deprived backgrounds and need the security of their own classroom and a sympathetic but firm teacher. About 20% of the children are obviously going to be delinquents—indeed some of them already are. Violence and bullying are commonplace and no child will complain about the behaviour of another because they are afraid. At least three times a week parents come in to complain that their children are being bullied. So far the bulk of injuries have been bad bruising, black eyes and bleeding noses but one boy has had his arm broken.

I may be giving the impression that the school is a blackboard jungle which is not strictly true. We have some delightful children in our school whose education is suffering because the staff are spending more time trying to control the trouble-makers than they are on actual teaching. The language used by some of our children is really quite shocking. They abuse any teacher who tries to discipline them. In my first week I had chairs thrown at me and I lost count of the number of times I was told to

f—— off. Parents come and complain that their children are picking up bad language at school and ask if we cannot impose stronger discipline, but obviously this must come from the headmaster.

Certain of our more difficult children do attack members of the staff. Generally it is nothing more serious than kicking on the shins but we had a more serious incident when a teacher was kicked, bitten, scratched and punched under the jaw by a ten-year-old girl. Some of the gang feuds in school spill over and are carried on after school. The police have had to sort out several fights on the estate including a stabbing. One of our mothers attacked another mother in the cloakroom and we had to call the police to break up the trouble.

Staff turnover is another great problem. Obviously since our children are a bit difficult and unsettled, teachers do not put up with conditions for long and try to get out as soon as possible. At the moment three of our teachers are on tranquillizers and one suffers severely from migraine. The noise in the school is quite intolerable and upsets many of the children and the staff. One cannot teach in an atmosphere of noise and chaos. Because the school is overcrowded I now have a small class of 15 children in the staffroom. They love being in my class because it is so peaceful compared to the rest of the building.

When the school first opened it was well stocked and equipped, but a great deal of equipment 'disappeared' and we are now short of stock. This lack of stock coupled with the constant battle the staff have to maintain order means that we have a number of bored junior children who work off their excess energy by damaging the school. In an average week we get toilet locks ripped off, toilet-roll holders broken, books, word cards, pictures and art displays broken. We are also a target for the local vandals and in the twelve months I have been in the school we have an average of four break-ins per term and at least three dozen windows broken. Last Wednesday one of our former pupils broke in just for a look round. He didn't do any damage but on Thursday evening someone came in through the window he had broken, plugged all the sinks and turned on 36 taps and a shower. The school was flooded to a depth of four inches, the carpets were soaked and a lot of stock and equipment ruined. The head was off sick. We had no deputy as he was away on a course and there was no one person in authority. Fortunately the weather was good so we moved the children and furniture outside. By Tuesday of this week we were still waterlogged and the carpets were going mouldy and coming up off the floor. The deputy director of education closed the school, and had a long meeting with the staff. The carpets have been shampooed and treated with anti-mould compound, the school is now immaculate, cleaner and tidier than it has ever been and we are going to have the damaged stock replaced. The damage will cost hundreds of pounds but the flood could turn out to be a blessing in disguise. The education hierarchy are so concerned about our school they are giving us extra staff and talking about putting in walls and doors as they doubt the wisdom of having an open-plan school in a difficult area.

I do not believe all open-plan schools are a failure. My own children are doing very well in an open-plan school but they have a very strong head, an experienced and settled staff and children who come from a settled, middle-class environment. For children from a less fortunate environment open plan is disaster. They have enough problems to cope with when they come from big families where Dad is out of work, one-parent families, families where Dad is violent, where Mum cannot cope, where there is little or no stability in their life. They need a conventional school building where they can have the security of *their* classroom and *their* teacher, where one can build and develop a sense of loyalty and class spirit.

In my own school the appalling design causes half the problems. One expects that there will be difficulties in any overspill area where people are moved away from family and familiar surroundings but I am convinced our children would be much happier and feel more settled in a conventional building.

Class Teacher

Experiences in a London Comprehensive

Teachers do not leave London schools just because of inadequate salaries or conditions in the normal sense. Young teachers like myself are leaving, although we are highly qualified and even successful, as far as we can judge, with some pupils. We are leaving because we need to practise our profession in a situation in which we are supported both inside and outside the school.

One of my major difficulties on entering the comprehensive school where I was to start my teaching career was the feeling of isolation which I met. From the time when I attended the school in May for an interview, I was left almost entirely to my own devices and given very little real or useful help or advice from my seniors. My interview was a hasty and superficial affair—which was not entirely unintentional—since if I had been in that environment a little longer and had had more time to think, or had I been less inexperienced, I might have recognized the signs of disorganization and declined to accept the post. However, I was fresh from college and as a member of the I.L.E.A. assigned staff, I had been sent to this school, full of missionary zeal (and I was going to need it) to meet the head and his staff and both look at the school and be looked over.

The interview was not what I expected it to be. In fact it was the first of a series of disillusionments which I was to encounter during my two years at the school. On my arrival, I was directed to the deputy head's office. I spent a very hurried ten or fifteen minutes with the deputy head, who seemed to be a fairly understanding person, but was quite obviously overburdened with work. Eighteen months later she suffered a nervous breakdown and was forced to resign and will probably never return to teaching. After a rapid briefing session concerning the school system and its general procedure, I was rushed from her office to the staffroom. In the corridor I was introduced, in passing, to the headmaster. This man seemed to be totally confused by the general situation in which he found himself in his own school, and, indeed, he retired prematurely two terms later after a series of illnesses. Although I did manage to consult this head twice during my first term (much more by my own dogged determination than by his availability), I have never met his successor, despite some effort on my part!

In the staffroom I met the then head of the English department, who resigned one month later. On inquiring about a syllabus, I was told that there was 'no syllabus. We tend to teach on our own personality.' All very well for those with a few years' teaching experience and a sufficiently strong personality to quell thirty rebellious teenagers with a look—but disastrous for a very 'green' probationer in a large London school. In fact, we inherited from this teacher a generation of pupils who could write marvellously expressive poetry, but could quite clearly not write anything verging on grammatically correct or fluent English—an imbalance which I hold to be a serious problem and which was also reflected in the general ethos of the school (i.e. too much freedom. Some self-discipline is necessary if we are to live communal lives.)

The question of availability of text books also caused problems; it seemed it was largely a matter of who got to the book cupboard first. Throughout my career at the school there was a battle raging over books. If books were allowed to be taken home for homework or further study, they rarely reappeared in school. Hence, pupils were not allowed to take books home. Then a further problem arose for those who wanted to study for exams. On one occasion we were so short of C.S.E. set books and there was no money available for new ones, that I had to go out and buy twenty copies of *Animal Farm* at my own expense, and loan them out to my fifth form. The book cupboard was never very well stocked because a large proportion of our yearly requisition consisted of replacement copies of set books for those already damaged or lost. Consequently, little money was left over to be spent on books for the lower school.

Stock—stationery, pencils, rulers, etc.—was also like gold-dust, and many senior teachers who had keys to the stock-cupboard would hoard it accordingly.

After my interview with the head of department, I was officially appointed, and was shown out of the school with a promise that my timetable would be sent to me during the summer. In fact, it wasn't.

On taking up my post in September, I found that no new head of department had been appointed. We lacked direction from the beginning; the general climate in the staffroom was one of survival rather than real educational achievement. Our department remained without a head for my first two terms, and when one did finally arrive the strain proved too much for him, and he resigned on medical advice before the term was out.

In addition to there being no syllabus, I was given no detailed information or accounts of what material had been covered by the classes I was to take, and I had to gather what information I could from the classes concerned. Also on my first day I discovered that I was to be a first-year form teacher. It came as something of a surprise—although it had been hinted at during my interview. This meant that for the first few days, certainly, the only person that these newcomers felt they could turn to with their worries, problems and queries was myself. This involved a certain amount of bluffing on my part—a skill which, of necessity, became quite highly developed during my stay there. The responsibility of my own class was one which, for the most part, I enjoyed and valued, but it became rather burdensome on the occasions—especially during my first days and weeks—when I, in my need for similar reassurance at a different level, was not being given it.

In fact, the actual advice and help that I received during my early days at the school was minimal. The deputy head had said that she would always be available, but, of course, this was not so. What is more, when one is inexperienced and in one's first job, one is loath to keep running to the deputy head. I really missed the support of a head of department for all sorts of advice—curricular, disciplinary and administrative. The head offered little useful assistance. His advice consisted of light-hearted quips which were either simple common sense or had become totally irrelevant in the passage of time since his own early days of teaching. This lack of support was also reflected by the administrators at County Hall. Apparently, every 'London first appointment' is supposed to be assigned to a supervisor to whom he or she can turn if in need of help or advice; but I, and others like me in this and other schools, never met or heard from such a person. No inspector ever visited me in school, and I passed my probationary year without anyone entering my classes in a supervisory capacity. I could have been teaching *anything* to my pupils.

In my second year, when I had been experiencing a lot of trouble with one particular class and had received no help from all the proper channels, I asked if I could have an English inspector come in to see me with that class, in the hope that he might be able to help. He did come, he attended the wrong lesson (a first-year class with no problems)—he made a few condescending and patronizing remarks and disappeared. The following day I informed my head of department that I would be leaving at the first opportunity. It was the ultimate step in a culmination of refusals to recognize a growing situation of disrespect and indiscipline during which I had been constantly refused help and support by those reputed to be capable of offering it, and I had taken enough.

Of course, what has happened to me, and others like me, is comparable to the effect of this system on the more intelligent pupils and on those who, despite the system, are anxious to learn. I have repeatedly experienced situations in which I see a child struggling to learn and educate himself against overwhelming odds. There have even been occasions when pupils have asked me for extra, individual lessons in their lunch hour because they cannot concentrate during lessons. I also used to teach a child who asked me if she could do her schoolwork for me at home—because she wanted to do it properly and she said she could never work well in school—'too much noise, Miss'. What an indictment of the school ethos! This pupil was, of course, an exception. Many others, finding themselves unable to compete against the pervading atmosphere, find that they cannot cope with the situation and they simply give up and withdraw into themselves and, in consequence, tragically under-achieve. I am more fortunate. I can at least physically remove myself from the environment and find an alternative; but the pupils must live with it, at least until they are fifteen.

My training—although academically and socially very rewarding—did not equip me for this sort of school; in fact, it bore no relation to it whatever. Curriculum lectures were too few and too inadequate, and classroom management as such is in my opinion really unteachable. My two teaching practices were in fairly tough schools in Peterborough and Stevenage, but even so, they were in a different world. Furthermore I was very closely supervised and was given a great deal of help from my tutors. I think there is much to be said in favour of the final year's training taking the form of an 'in-training' period, during which the probationary teacher is quite closely supervised and knows that he or she has support which is clearly available, if needed. However, this is still useless if the schools are too large, and badly run and led.

I feel that the teaching role should be, to a certain extent, a shared, co-operative role with a staff forming a team of people led by the head, all working together to a common purpose. Such co-operation is essential in the present educational system and its tragic absence certainly accounts for much of the solitariness and nervous and physical exhaustion which have confronted many young teachers, myself included. In my opinion, the weakening of the important web of human relationships in schools may be largely accounted for by the recent popular theory that 'Big is Beautiful' and is necessarily good. The vast increase in the size of schools (my own had approximately 1,300 pupils on roll, and was small in comparison with many comprehensive schools) has the inevitable consequence in many schools of depersonalization and the gradual disintegration of a notion of a common, unifying purpose. Such a feeling of displacement and lack of immediacy will tend to result in the frequent 'breakdowns of communication'—a phrase which has become a scapegoat for inefficiency in an institution which has become too large to cope with the very personal task of educating the young. I think we have reached a significantly sad state of affairs when a fifteen-year-old pupil speaks to me of his headmaster as 'that voice over the tannoy'. Instead of a disembodied voice, the head should provide a lead and a sense of purpose to both teachers and pupils alike. Too often, as in my own experience, the head has become a distant, shadowy and inaccessible figure. Where there is a lack of meaningful relationships at the top, so there will often be a similar absence in the staffroom. There will be no real teamwork, and, faced with increasingly difficult classes and little or no structure of discipline and support from more experienced members of staff, there will be a feeling of role-alienation and frustration, and a high turnover rate of teaching staff will result. Consequently the pupils have no time to form useful relationships with their teachers, and they become unmanageable. Such a situation, with a more diverse curriculum which depends greatly on pupil-teacher interaction, is tragic. It is precisely this situation which met me on entering a London comprehensive school, and it is becoming increasingly widespread.

I remember an occasion in my first term when a young supply teacher was faced with controlling, for 70 minutes, a class of unruly fifth years who happened to be in the classroom opposite to mine. She was, understandably, quite unable to manage them, and she followed the correct procedure by sending a plea for assistance to the head of the fifth year. The note was duly returned with an addendum from the appropriate head of year, saying that he would discuss this with her at break. That teacher needed immediate help, and it was denied her; this type of behaviour was not unusual where I taught, and in similar schools where my friends taught.

I could add to this a further experience of my own. In my first year in the school I was given an English class of twenty school-leavers, most of whom could hardly read or write. Not one of these youngsters was even slightly interested in school; indeed, one lad who had truanted from my lesson and whom I subsequently met in the downstairs corridor five minutes later, smoking a cigarette, answered my query about the reason for his absence from an English lesson a few minutes earlier with: 'Don't be daft, Miss, you know I only come to school to meet me friends.' It was the antics and the abuse directed at me by this class which led me, having found no support from various other channels, namely the head of department, the form tutors, the year head and the deputy head, eventually to approach the headmaster for assistance. Having listened to my story of the abuse and disrespect which I had been receiving at the hands of these young hooligans, the head turned to me and offered me the following piece of devastating advice: 'Yes, but you do realize Miss . . . that your standards are rather high. I think your best line of action would be to lower your standards.'

This lack of communication was also experienced by the pupils in relation to the head. Full school assemblies were rarely held in the school where I taught—there was approximately one per term—but when such an assembly was held, it was usually beyond the understanding or interest of the majority of the children.

The school alone is by no means responsible for the nihilistic behaviour of many pupils. The home environment remains the most powerful influence in the development of the child, and the responsibility for the growing wilfulness and ineducability of modern youth can, in most cases, be laid at the feet of the parents. In most homes in the area of London where I taught the children ruled their parents, thus becoming over-indulged and selfish. I believe that until we have some legal means of enforcing parental responsibility for a child's actions, the problem will remain and schools will be relatively powerless in dealing with miscreants. I think that, in the case of a pupil who has become completely uncontrollable in school, we should adopt a system like that in New Zealand, where the offender is denied admittance to the school and is sent home to be cared for by his parents and is no longer a responsibility to the school. I think that if this were to happen, the child would in many cases (and I do not mean in cases of severe maladjustment, etc.) soon come to his senses and sort himself out, and the teacher and the rest of the class would be able to get on with the real business of education. Until such a time we must not be surprised to hear remarks directed at the teacher such as: 'Don't you tell *me* what to do. I'll get me Dad after you.' And, when asked to pick up a piece of litter he himself had dropped: '*You* pick it up, I'm not a bloody scrubber.'

The list of problems which I, and others like me, have to face in schools today is never-ending. The decline of the values of care and community, the effects upon children of a hedonistic culture, a growing disrespect for learning within institutions which are far too big and impersonal— all these generate a nihilism in which children find no source of those values by which one should respect others and give service to a community. In such a situation it is impossible to uphold a respect for study, for that collaboration which education essentially is. Consequently, teachers find that they simply cannot teach; for many young teachers the feeling of failure and the futility of their efforts become overwhelming. They find their position in school morally untenable and they resign from their posts, and, increasingly often, leave the profession entirely. I am one of the many who have fallen foul of this drastic situation and I have decided, after struggling for two years, to direct my talents in a different direction. To use an immediate example of the wastage of trained teachers from our schools, witness myself and my four friends. Five of us— all with good degrees and certificates of education—came to London in September 1972 to teach in London schools. Out of these five young women, one has become a research assistant at a famous American university, another has become a secretary, and two more have left teaching in England and may go to Europe to teach. All have sworn never to teach in London again, unless there is massive reorganization in the school situation there.

Young Teacher

Examinations: Seven Questions

C. B. COX

All examinations need to be constantly scrutinized, and methods improved. An examination may force students to confine attention to too narrow a field, or it may be used too rigidly for selection purposes. Careful research needs to be undertaken into ways in which examinations can be made more accurate as guides to ability.

But although examinations are never perfect they are an essential part of an education system. There are powerful arguments for public examinations which most opponents choose to ignore. Those who attack examinations are often educationalists of the kind described by Bernice Martin in 'The Mining of the Ivory Tower' (pp. 52–59): those who have withdrawn themselves from the world of productive work, from the needs of social reality.

These are the questions that opponents of examinations need to answer:

1   If there are no public examinations, what happens when a student applies for a job?
There are two possible replies:
(*a*) 'He will be supported by a reference from his teachers.'
But teachers are inconsistent in their gradings. One school may mark 20% higher than another. The employer will receive no reliable information.
(*b*) 'Firms can set their own exams.'
But this will mean that instead of one examination, the student will have to take several. Imagine the plight of the third-year university student, passing from a tough examination at I.C.I. to a similar test at Courtaulds to another one at Cadbury Schweppes. If he failed these, he would have to start off on a round of further exams. Consider all the extra work this would involve for industry.

2   If there are no public examinations, will not this reduce the chances of a working-class boy or girl, and shift us back to the abuses of the old-boy network?
This is an argument which opponents of examinations are particularly afraid of mentioning. When he applies for a job, a working-class student can at present bring forward certificates to prove his competence. This has enabled thousands of working-class children to succeed in the professions and in industry. Without exams selection committees will inevitably prefer the middle-class applicant from a well-known school.

33

3 If there are no public exams, how will parents find out about schools with low standards?

Already the achievements of primary schools in teaching reading and numeracy vary enormously. Now there is no 11+ examination, there is no adequate check on attainment. Parents may remain unaware for years that their children are falling behind. This is why in our Letter to M.P.s and Parents we advocate national tests of achievement. Exams test the efficiency of the teacher and teaching systems.

4 Without exams, what guarantee is there for the public that a doctor or architect or accountant or teacher is competent?

In a complicated society, most of us are not in a position to judge whether a specialist is qualified. Passing exams before entering a profession is, thus, a necessary protection for the public.

5 Without public exams, what control is left over the subjects taught in schools?

Today many secondary schools are offering children a mish-mash of sociology and politics instead of traditional study of past history and literature. These 'inter-disciplinary', 'relevant' courses are often heavily influenced by the teachers' own opinions. Teachers do not say 'Vote Communist or International Socialist' in their lessons, but they do suggest that capitalism and competition are evil. Public examinations force teachers to cover areas of study which general educated opinion in Britain believes appropriate for children. If there are no syllabuses laid down by the needs of public exams, children may be submitted to all kinds of eccentric courses, and parents will find out too late.

6 If examinations are replaced by continuous assessment, will this not damage the proper relationship between teacher and student?

The unreliability of teacher assessment has already been mentioned. In systems of continuous assessment, no external examiner has the time to scrutinize adequately the piles of essays and projects, and comparability between one school and another becomes impossible. But, equally important, continuous assessment sours personal relationships. Teachers can never be sure if a student is telling the whole truth, or covering up weaknesses. Students are forced to curry favour, and must conform to the ideas of their teachers. It is more difficult for them to be independent. Is this really what student radicals want? Abolishing exams puts students under the dictatorship of teacher assessment.

7 Is there any evidence that the average adolescent will work hard at school at difficult subjects without the incentive of examinations?

Discipline in America

RICHARD PECK

There is a long tradition in America of passing the blame for our undisciplined young. Teachers condemn parents. Parents cite Dr Spock. And everyone decries the vast technologies and dislocations of a continually urbanizing nation. Even as smug and ubiquitous a technology as television comes under attack:

> Television, like films and the theatre, ought to be an adult medium of entertainment, if only because it subverts the natural authority of parents.[1]

No-one is equal to tracing the subversion of the natural authority of adults in our society. Schools have shifted from towers of academic and personal discipline to the very arenas of revolt and crime. The pioneer-era teacher who could dispense discipline and sudden justice all over a small town is now lost in megalopolis.

It is easy to sentimentalize over our rural past, and not very instructive. The most vivid paradigm of the state of discipline in the mid-1970s is the large urban school. Its problems sweep the country, and fleeing families take the problems with them. The television news camera is no longer as fixated upon student revolt as it was in the 1960s. The abolition of military conscription and the end of Vietnam war involvement have tranquillized older adolescents. Now that rebellion is no longer clothed in ideology except to a degree in racial matters, problems of discipline and mere survival, particularly among younger children, are not adequately aired.

The problems of the permissively reared persist. And schools persist in dealing with them by indirection and by unwisely divorcing the challenges of personal discipline from academic discipline. As a pivotal example, at a time when most schoolchildren cannot read their textbooks, schools continue to attempt expensive innovations to make education a more relaxed and undirected pastime.

Enormous urban schools receive the worst marks for truancy, illiteracy, and racial and gang warfare. Given their extreme condition, the impulse to humanize them is understandable. But the approach is permissive, aiming at placating rather than teaching. And the reforming of a secondary school that may well have 4,000 students on a double shift runs foul of bureaucracy.

One attempt to make education more intimate is the mini-school plan. Selected students are assigned to 'the unstructured setting' of small schools-within-schools with discussion groups and lounges. The emphasis is on giving students a point of identity, but no additional time is offered for academic learning.

One observer, Diane Divoky, excoriates traditional teachers for force-feeding subject matter, but she criticizes the mini-school too:

> Students could smoke in the available lounges, but not where it counted—in the classrooms. No one considered operating on a first-name basis. Bells and 'official

[1] William V. Shannon, 'What Code of Values Can We Teach Our Children Now?' *The New York Times Magazine*, 16 January 1972.

periods' in which school business was transacted . . . were eliminated for the first few days, but complaints from the staff about the lack of order got them rapidly reinstated. (Bells keyed to the schedules of various mini-schools soon began to ring throughout the school every few minutes, a surrealistic situation that was finally brought under control by extensive administrative memos about the 'bells problem.') [2]

Critics troubled about adequate smoking places appear less concerned with crimes of violence by students against their peers and teachers. Nor is the individual student's frustrated desire for order and learning much noted. Inner-city schools have had ample opportunity to learn the disappointing result of a totally relaxed school atmosphere. The young prefer to relax elsewhere—and do.

The truancy problem is a somewhat oblique disciplinary concern. Whole school systems are predicated on the certainty that a significant percentage of the students will be absent. If they all showed up, there wouldn't be room for them. A recent survey revealed that 200,000 of the 1.2 million New York City students are absent every day, a figure that does not include those who report for roll call and then vanish.

Again it is the urban system where the problem is especially severe. The decentralizing of school board authority into neighbourhood autonomies has decreased the numbers and effectiveness of 'attendance teachers' (once called truant officers). In New York City there are 20% fewer attendance teachers now than in 1969, and the Board of Education is asking for 2.5 million dollars to increase their numbers.[3]

The crimes committed by truants who travel in packs are often regarded by schools as beyond their jurisdiction. The diminished numbers of attendance teachers weaken the link between school and community. Parents are thus rarely called to account.

A problem never aired is that many youngsters absent themselves from school out of fear of their peers. The focus remains on catering to the psychological needs of the troublesome with a residue of contempt for the victim, an accurate approximation of adult life in America.

The tendency to regroup children rather than to deal directly with their behaviour problems is evident in the fairly recent trend toward middle schools. Traditionally children of 13–16 years attend junior high schools. The newer middle-school plan groups them in the 12–14 age group. An underlying idea is that the oldest of the junior-high students often provide bad behaviour examples and prey upon the younger.

The point is more diplomatically made by a middle-school principal in a Long Island suburban town. Mario Di Sciullo says,

I don't feel the junior high school has any validity any more, from the sole point of view that 9th-graders set an example that is too advanced in social behaviour for 7th- and 8th-graders to deal with. . . . Children in grades 6 through 8 experience rapid and irregular growth. They are erratic and unpredictable. . . . All our activities are geared to satisfying their needs—physical, academic and emotional—and dealing with their outbursts and successes.[4]

Mr Di Sciullo does not explain how his middle school deals with outbursts, but he reports that 'academic progress is pretty successful' and that attendance has improved 'close to 200%'. One of his neighbouring colleagues says

more flatly: 'We wanted our students out of the high school.' Delaying contact with older students is surely a questionable method of dealing with the youngest adolescents. Perhaps its chief effect is a construction spate of 'open-plan' buildings, a windfall to building contractors in this age of declining school enrolment and tight money.

'Open-plan' school architecture is not limited to middle-school construction. But it is another legacy of the 1960s era of easy funding and group-behaviour experimentalism. The wall-less 'learning areas' grouped fluidly around a central 'resource centre' became a fad for schools in the United States and Canada. From 1967 to 1972 Ontario constructed 400 'open-area' schools, 10% of all the schools in the province.

The use of architecture to dispel conventional classroom rigidity is turning out to be difficult to live with. The noise militates against literacy training. The play space promises fun and games. In order to create a semblance of the coherent classroom, teachers have erected temporary walls and in one notable instance raised a tent.

Since the open plan has been particularly popular for elementary schools, the children begin their schooling in a chaotic atmosphere where they observe teachers struggling for order and where they find distractions sanctioned.

A phenomenon of the 1970s is the mildly militant teacher. Though a well-publicized surfeit of teachers diminishes most political influence, unionized teachers are organizing for specific security measures.

Liberal, middle-class suburban communities are reluctant to post policemen in school corridors. But in 1972 the New York City United Federation of Teachers requested a contract to provide security guards assigned to all secondary schools at a ratio of one guard to every 175 students and to all elementary schools at a ratio of one guard to every 250 students. This would have required 6,000 guards instead of the existing 200. An additional proposal called for 'school district attorneys' to relieve administrators of the need to press charges against pupils (and presumably non-pupils) who commit crimes or disruptive acts on school property.

The Board of Education's counter-proposal created 200 'school service officers' to replace the existing guards, under the direction of a safety director who was a former police commander in the Harlem district. The limitations of the new plan were made clear by Chancellor Harvey Scribner who described the authority of the school service officers:

. . . the objective is to place trained people in the schools who can work constructively with students and staff to make the schools less prone to incidents, and who can cope rationally and effectively with incidents when they occur.[5]

However effective a school police force might be, it would be sadly crippled by juvenile court authorities who rarely remove a criminal youngster from society, even temporarily.

Coping rationally with irrational acts, dealing on respectful terms with gang leaders, failing to press charges against schoolhouse drug dealers, deferring to minority-group pressures for preferential treatment, relaxing the academic and behavioural expectations for the young, continue to disfigure this decade.

It is significant that constructive ideas for improved discipline do not fill the pages of the professional journals of various subject areas. Curriculum planners have the evidence of the failure of ethnic studies programmes,

[2] *Saturday Review*, 18 December 1971.
[3] *The Christian Science Monitor*, 29 March 1974.
[4] *The New York Times*, 7 July 1974.

[1]*The New York Times*, 30 July 1972.

remedial reading materials, and contemporary, youth-centred subject matter. History, foreign language, and forensics have all but vanished from school curricula, denying the young those specific disciplines. In English, composition is largely optional, and shorter, more popular readings are assigned (or suggested) to accommodate unstretched attention spans.

Until classroom teachers organize to insist upon raised standards, the discipline of foreign language for all students, and rigid end-of-year examinations, students will continue to act out their aggressions against an adult authority that provides them with neither challenge nor security.

Schools have never lived so far from parents as they now do. Parents are transferring their children from tax-supported schools to burgeoning private schools that need offer very little more than physical safety. Only sweeping reforms and widespread removal of youthful criminals from the school will bring back urban and suburban middle-class families to a support for local schools. But there is at this moment little real evidence of such an organized and inevitably controversial movement.

Educational Statistics

C. B. COX

In the House of Commons on 1 May 1974, Mr Prentice stated that 'the results in comprehensive schools have been at least as good as, if not better than, those in grammar schools', and then on 3 July he claimed that there was statistical evidence to support his belief that the introduction of comprehensive education was raising standards. I would contend that this claim constitutes a serious misrepresentation of the facts.

Quite often the newspapers include accounts of research which purports to show that the examination results of comprehensive schools are better than those in areas which still maintain the old grammar/technical/secondary modern school divisions. Such research has never stood up to serious investigation by qualified statisticians, and is really just propaganda.

The public is being deceived. Politicians are being deceived. We are not saying that the supporters of comprehensive schools who publish these statistics are liars. They are often naïve, well-intentioned people easily led by the nose. They only come to grips with reality when their own children are involved. They then ensure that their offspring are selected for good comprehensives, or, as in several notorious recent cases, send them off to independent or direct grant schools. If supporters of comprehensive education want the truth, let them join the Black Paper editors in demanding a government inquiry into standards in schools. This should be carried out by impartial investigators, not by active campaigners for or against the new schemes. Some comprehensives are good. Let us find out which they are, and what methods they are adopting. Some are very bad. Parents have a right to know to what kinds of institution their children are being sent.

Professor Robin Pedley and Dr Guy Neave

After Mr Prentice's 1 May statement in the Commons, a statistician wrote to the Minister to ask for justification of the claim that comprehensive schools were producing results at least as good as those of grammar schools. The spokesman for the Department of Education and Science who replied quoted the Robin Pedley 1968 figures published in his book, *The Comprehensive School* (1969). No other figures were brought forward as evidence. This is astonishing. First, Pedley's book was five years old, and it is amazing that no new figures had been prepared. More important, Pedley's calculations were discredited long ago, and it is strange that the people advising Mr Prentice seemed unaware of this.

The main attack on Pedley's figures, when they first appeared, was written by John Todd, who is at present doing research in mathematics at Cambridge. His article was published in *Black Paper Three* in 1970. As Professor Pedley's figures are still regarded as authoritative by many comprehensivists, and have been extensively quoted, it's worth repeating Todd's main arguments:

The first point to make clear, when talking about Professor Pedley's survey, is that the schools which it covered were not representative of comprehensives in general. He only considered results from schools which had been founded for at least seven years, and which took 90% or more of the children from their area. He did this in an attempt to estimate the probable performance of a fully comprehensive State system of schools; but it meant that his sample covered only 67 of the national total of 745 comprehensive schools in 1968.

The second fact which should be noticed is that his results are not valid as an indicator of the effects of national comprehensive education. His results are drawn from answers to a questionnaire which he sent to comprehensive schools, and to which only 73% of the schools replied. For so emotionally and politically charged a question as the examination performance of comprehensive schools, a question asked of those schools by a researcher nationally famous as their champion, one would not be surprised if the schools which replied had more favourable results than those which did not. Certainly one cannot assume that the results reported were representative of those of all comprehensives of the type surveyed.

Another point is that the schools surveyed by Professor Pedley were very unevenly distributed over the country. He excluded from his survey all comprehensives in the Inner London Education Authority (I.L.E.A.), although 66 of them had been founded for at least seven years, 'because of the difficulty of defining satisfactorily their degree of comprehensiveness'.[1] The result was that the 67 schools in his survey contained only one school in the Greater London Council area, though this area contains 15% of national secondary

[1] *The Comprehensive School* (1969 edition), p. 101.

school children, against 24 schools in Wales, which contains only 6%.[2] Nor was there a fair balance in the types of area from which the schools drew; 41 of the schools were in country towns (22 of them in Wales), against only 26 in cities, suburbs and industrial conurbations, though the latter contain by far the greater part of the population.

It is clear from the above account that Professor Pedley's results cannot validly be compared with the national results from other types of school. Nevertheless, Professor Pedley invited readers of his book to compare his results with the national figures for State-maintained schools (i.e. schools other than direct grant and independent schools).

Immediately after the publication of *Black Paper Two* its critics duly started to flourish Professor Pedley's figures, along with the latest results from all maintained schools. The comprehensives, they claimed, had 20.1% of pupils leaving with five or more 'O' level passes, against 17.6% from maintained schools; for two or more 'A' levels, the respective figures were 9.7% and 9.2%.[3] The Chairman of the Comprehensive Schools Committee wrote: 'the comprehensive performance is impressive'.[4] But not only had these critics accepted the validity of Professor Pedley's results; they had biased the comparison itself. Whereas the Pedley figures were for school leavers in the academic year 1967/8, the maintained school results were for the year before. The maintained school results for 1967/8, which have since been published, show an improvement to 9.6% of leavers having two or more 'A' levels.

Furthermore Professor Pedley counted a grade 1 pass at C.S.E. as being an 'O' level pass; this was not done for the maintained school results, which also excluded 'O' level passes awarded on 'A' level papers. When this is also allowed for, the proportion of maintained school leavers obtaining five or more 'O' level passes rises to 18.9%.[5]

In short Professor Pedley's figures do not stand up to close scrutiny. Yet comprehensive propagandists did everything they could to persuade those concerned with education that the comparison was of prime importance in assessing the examination performance of comprehensive schools.

Dr Neave's analysis of comprehensive schools

Mr Prentice's statements were probably also influenced by articles in the press in January 1974 describing figures supplied by Dr Guy Neave of the Sociology of Education Unit, Edinburgh University, and published in the journal of the Campaign for Comprehensive Education. Caroline Benn wrote that these statistics 'prove beyond doubt that comprehensive schools not only maintain standards, but in the case of university entry, improve upon them well beyond what might have been expected'. Neave's material was published in the *Guardian*—without criticism—on 8 January 1974.

Dr Neave pointed out that in the years 1966–71 the number of comprehensive sixth-formers going to university increased nearly five and a half times. The increase in the number of pupils entering comprehensive schools in these six years was just over three and a half times. The number going to university from comprehensives—as a percentage of total entry—rose during the six years from 5.9% to 28.4%. While the grammar school entrants had decreased to 88% of the 1966 total, the comprehensive school proportion had increased by 487%.

[2] *Statistics of Education 1968* Vol. 1 (H.M.S.O., 1969), Table 2.
[3] *Sunday Times*, 12 October 1969.
[4] Letter to *The Spectator*, 8 November 1969.
[5] *Statistics of Education 1968* Vol. 2 (H.M.S.O., 1970), Table 19.

The Times Educational Supplement published a report on this material on 11 January. On 25 January several letters appeared in the *T.E.S.* pointing out the fallacies in Neave's arguments. But by this time the damage was done. The public had been misled. Mr Prentice had been misled.

Dr Neave's figures cover a period when large numbers of grammar schools were turned into comprehensives. Obviously during such a time the number of entrants to universities from comprehensives must go up sharply, as grammars become comprehensives, and to claim this as a triumph for the comprehensives is absurd.

Secondly, there is no relevance in comparing the number of children leaving comprehensives and going to university in a particular year with the number entering comprehensives in the same year. Many comprehensives in 1971 were recently grammar schools, and the results of their children can hardly be used as meaningful in relation to pupils entering comprehensives at the same time.

The ratio of university entrants to numbers of leavers gives a far better indication of academic attainment. In 1969, 1970, 1971 and 1972 (the latest year for which statistics are available) the proportion of comprehensive school leavers going on to university was 3.4%, 3.8%, 3.6% and 3.6%. The grammar schools' percentages during this period were 18.8%, 18.5%, 18.8% and 17.9% respectively. Even the combined grammar schools and secondary moderns percentage is about $5\frac{1}{8}$% in 1972, whilst the all-maintained schools figure is 4.4%. The 1972 D.E.S. statistics indicate broadly comparable results in respect of the comprehensive system and of the selective system at the lower levels of educational attainment, but the comprehensives are *bettered* by the combined grammar and secondary moderns by 15% in numbers of students with five or more 'O' levels, 29% in numbers of students with one or more 'A' levels, and 42% with two or more 'A' levels.

It may justly be argued that the comprehensives include many 'sink' schools which are no more than huge secondary moderns, creamed off by grammar and direct grant schools. But these figures make nonsense of Dr Neave's claim that the case for comprehensive education can be supported by statistics.

The Manchester Comprehensives

On 19 July 1974 the *T.E.S.* published on its front page details of a report on 'O' level results in Manchester maintained county and voluntary schools in the years 1964 to 1973. This report has been given proper publicity, and was quoted by Norman St John Stevas during the 1974 Autumn Election campaign. The statistics were prepared by the Chief Education Officer. Since comprehensive reorganization in 1967 the proportion of Manchester schoolchildren going in for G.C.E. 'O' levels has been falling sharply. A leader in the *T.E.S.* commented:

> The *prima facie* case is, however, that going comprehensive in Manchester has been followed (not necessarily as cause and effect) by a drop in the percentage of the age group taking 'O' levels in the reorganized county schools, while in the separate Roman Catholic grammar and modern schools the percentage has forged ahead, from a lower base to the point where it is now greater than in the county schools.

The comprehensive lobby has argued that, although standards in Manchester comprehensives have gone down, this does not mean they will continue to do so. In contrast, Manchester teachers to whom we have talked suggest that as we proceed through the 1970s the situation will worsen as the old grammar school influences are forgotten.

On 25 October 1974 Sheffield published figures in the

T.E.S purporting to show that standards in their comprehensives were being maintained. Unfortunately for Sheffield a close examination of their results showed that the number of 'O' level passes per pupil was lower than the national average.

Fred Naylor

In his article, 'Comprehensive Mythology' (pp. 20–24), Fred Naylor draws attention to the fact that achievements at 'A' level are significantly below the projections on which the government based their earlier forecasts of student expansion through the seventies. The *T.E.S.* reported on 1 February 1974 that 92,500 students (of all kinds) got at least two 'A' levels in 1971, compared with the projection in the 1970 Education Planning Paper of 100,500. Similarly, 93,400 got two or more 'A' levels in 1972, compared with the projection of about 102,000. In addition, Mr Naylor points out that the expected increase of 40% in the number of school leavers with two or more 'A' level passes, between 1965 and 1972, turned out in practice to be one of only 23%. Why has this happened? A variety of reasons might be put forward. It seems very possible that comprehensive reorganization had something to do with this shortfall.

Mr Naylor also deals with the National Foundation of Educational Research *Achievement in Mathematics* and *A Critical Appraisal of Comprehensive Education*. Both provide evidence of lower standards of attainment in comprehensive schools.

We also know that the percentage of open awards at Oxbridge won from comprehensives fell between 1970 and 1972, despite the fact that the number of pupils attending such schools increased by over 30%.

The Percentile

The newspapers often carry reports about the increases in the number of school leavers with five 'O' levels or one 'A' level. In the decade up to 1972 the number of school leavers with at least five G.C.E. 'O' levels has increased from 15% to 23% of the age groups, and with at least one 'A' level from 9% to 16%. We are delighted that more students are staying on at school and succeeding in passing examinations. We wonder whether the increases in the last few years might not have been very much greater if ill-judged comprehensive schemes had not been rushed through.

But there is one aspect of this increase which receives little comment in educational circles, and is unknown to many parents, teachers and politicians. The examining boards pass roughly the same percentage in the major subjects every year. In Appendix F of the third report of the Secondary Schools Examination Council (predecessor of the present Schools Council), *Examinations in Secondary Schools: the General Certificate of Education and Sixth Form Studies* (H.M.S.O. 1960) it was laid down that, in general, the percentage of entries to achieve the various grades at 'A' levels should be as follows: Grade A—10%, Grade B—15%, Grade C—10%, Grade D—15%, Grade E—20%. This means a 70% pass rate. Although the boards apply the system with some discretion and flexibility, so that quite pronounced departures from the prescribed norms may be found in atypical and small-entry subjects, under their present terms of reference the boards may not depart significantly from the norms in the main 'A' level subjects offered by large numbers of candidates. A similar system ensures that about 60% pass 'O' level every year. The belief is that with a large entry there will not be great changes in the numbers passing from year to year, and that any discrepancies may reveal a change in the standards of examiners. This may operate in normal times, but are the times normal?

In the period from 1960 to 1972 the number of students passing 'A' level English in the summer examinations increased from 14,565 to 44,131, in 'A' level French from 10,277 to 17,393, in chemistry from 16,605 to 23,736, and in geography from 7,665 to 22,763. In each case this represented roughly 70% of the entry, and, as has been stressed, the boards are not allowed to fail significantly more than 30%. In 'O' level English language the passes from 1960 to 1972 went up from 141,326 to 213,659 and in English literature from 94,876 to 136,414. The pass rate remained at roughly 60%.

These figures need careful analysis. Rises in the birth rate have to be considered. There are differences between subjects. The numbers passing French 'A' level are now falling (in spite of primary school French). But one thing sticks out clearly. In a period of twelve years, the numbers taking 'A' level English, to take the obvious example, have trebled. Are these normal times? Is it possible that in such a period of rapid expansion, the 70% who passed in 1972 are of roughly the same standard as the 70% who passed in 1960? It seems unlikely. It is tempting to deduce that as more and more students have been put in for the examination, the standard has declined. In a situation of this kind, there is often little difference between one year and the next, but over a period of time there is a slow drift downwards.

In conversation we have been told that on one occasion recently the pass mark for one board in a science subject fell to 28%, so that 70% might still pass. A secretary of an examining board is said to have complained that students with 58% in one subject were being awarded A's at 'A' level. Are these accounts true? The relation between examiners' marks and the actual number of passes is a secret kept by the examining boards. It is time that the whole matter was properly investigated and made available for public scrutiny.

University Statistics

A well-known argument against comprehensives is that in the less academic atmosphere of such schools bright children, particularly from the working classes, would have less inclination to go on to university. A feature of the last three years has been that the proportion of school leavers with good 'A' level passes who go to degree-level courses has been falling steadily. A reassessment of the probable total full-time student population in 1976/7 indicated an expected shortfall of between 8% and 11% below the national figure of 306,000 published in the 1972 Education White Paper. The latest U.C.C.A. statistics show that there is no longer fierce competition for university entry in many subjects, and that particularly in engineering, science and technology, students with very low grades are being accepted. In 1974 this trend continued, and in the social sciences students were being accepted with lower grades than ever before. The U.C.C.A. report of September 1974 shows that the number of serious applicants for university places exceeds the number of places available by only a small margin.

This situation has brought about a lowering of standards of entry in many departments (the notable exceptions are law and medicine). The universities depend for government financial support on high intakes, and in recent years have become increasingly desperate in their search for suitably qualified applicants. In 1973/4 the U.C.C.A. figures show a significant decrease in the number of students rejected before the 'A' level examinations were taken. Universities can no longer afford to maintain previous standards. Fifteen years ago the S.S.E.C. laid down that a B grade in 'A' level would be the usual qualification expected from a student proceeding to an Honours course. This has now been abandoned in most subjects.

On 11 October 1974 *The Times Higher Education Supplement* reported that a poll had discovered that a clear majority of Britain's more experienced academics believe that the average ability of students has declined since universities started to expand rapidly in the 1960s. Kingsley Amis was treated with contempt when he said that more will mean worse. Now increasing numbers of educationalists know he is being proved right. The problems of universities also derive from the bad image created by student troubles, and from publicity about lack of jobs for graduates. It is difficult to accept that lower standards are not also the result of comprehensive reorganization.

What is happening in polytechnics? Individual institutions have published information, but there is no national survey which can inform us about the numbers of students applying or their qualifications.

Conclusion

Thousands of pounds of government money are being spent on educational research. Much of it is trivial. Any research into a controversial area, if carried out by one person with his own prejudices and opinions, is likely to be biased. Yet with all this money available, we do not know the essential facts. Major government reports have been published in which the statistics give a false impression. The best-known example is the Plowden Report, which used the improvement in reading standards between 1948 and the mid-1960s as a triumphant vindication of 'progressive' methods. Its authors failed to realize that, because of evacuation and call-up of teachers during the war, standards in 1948 were particularly low. There was no evidence that standards in 1965 were any higher than in the 1930s, and the subsequent N.F.E.R. *The Trend of Reading Standards* (K. B. Start and B. K. Wells, 1972) showed a decline in reading standards of eleven-year-old pupils since 1964.

The Plowden statistics were quoted by highly influential people such as Mr Short and Sir Alec Clegg to support the growth of progressive education. Similarly, Robin Pedley's figures about comprehensive schools have greatly influenced politicians such as Mr Prentice. Yet these statistics were invalid. There is urgent need for the public to be properly informed. We must have a major government inquiry. If the Labour Party pushes ahead with the comprehensivization of schools before such an inquiry takes place, they will have proved they care more for dogma than for children.

Educational Consequences of Human Inequality

H. J. EYSENCK

It seems little more than common sense to say that educational programmes and methods should be derived from a realistic consideration of well-established facts. This, unfortunately, is not what is happening nowadays; 'facts' are invented to agree with preconceived ideological and political notions of what is desirable, and programmes are then based on these alleged 'facts'. Genetic differences leading to marked differences in ability and personality are well-established facts; I have surveyed the evidence both in a popular book (*The Inequality of Man*) and in two technical ones (*The Measurement of Intelligence* and *The Biological Basis of Personality*) and the conclusion which is forced on anyone who has studied the large amount of evidence now available is that these genetic differences are extremely powerful. As far as intelligence is concerned, most people interested in this field will by now be familiar with the estimate of 80% of the total variance being due to genetic causes, 20% to environmental ones; this estimate, which applies to western countries at the present time, may in fact be an underestimate of the contribution of genetic factors because society has become much more egalitarian since the majority of the studies in question took place, and greater egalitarianism must of course lead to a decline in the importance of environmental factors. Similarly, in the field of personality, the most important dimensions (extraversion-introversion and stability-neuroticism) show a heritability of something like 60%; this estimate is likely to be an underestimate because of the fact that personality cannot be as reliably measured as intelligence, and this lack of reliability is in effect subtracted from the heritability estimate.

These estimates are often decried by critics who seem to imagine that they are the outcome of arbitrary and illegitimate statistical exercises dreamed up by psychologists not too well acquainted with modern genetics. In fact, the methods of analysis were of course designed by geneticists, as may be seen in such books as *Biometrical Genetics* by K. Mathers and J. L. Jinks; and they have been applied by geneticists to data collected by psychologists. The estimates of heritability mentioned in the first paragraph of this article have in fact been taken from a very detailed paper by J. L. Jinks and D. Fulker, using these up-to-date methods of analysis to set up and test models of gene action in human behaviour. No doubt criticisms of these precise estimates are feasible; scientific measurements and estimates of this kind are all subject to errors, and consequently to improvement. What I think cannot be doubted is that these estimates are sufficiently near the true values to leave no doubt about the relevance of genetics to human behaviour, whether cognitive or emotional, whether social or pathological.

So much has been written about the inheritance of intelligence, and its relevance to education, that it may be more interesting to concentrate in this article a little more on personality. At first sight the fact that extraversion and neuroticism are strongly inherited may not strike the reader as very important, at least as far as education is concerned; however, there are many interesting links. First of all, there is a connection between these two personality traits and neurotic and antisocial behaviour; neurotics tend to be introverted and have unstable emotions, while criminals and antisocial people generally (including children who behave in an antisocial manner) tend to be extraverted and have unstable emotions. Both criminality and neurosis have a strong hereditary basis; for both, foster children tend to follow the example of their biological parents, not their foster parents, and for both, identical twins show far more concordance than do fraternal twins. (In other words, if one twin is neurotic or criminal, so will the other one be if they are identical; not if they are fraternal.)

Secondly, as far as education is concerned, it is well enough known that high I.Q. is a favourable sign for success; it is less well known that personality also plays an important part. It does so along three lines. In the first place, a high degree of neuroticism (emotional instability) is definitely harmful; students of this kind do much less well than those who are more stable. Similarly, extraverted students do less well than introverted ones, particularly at university (although the same trend can already be observed at secondary school). Extraverted and unstable students do worst of all; at university level, personality scales predict success rather better than do I.Q. tests (largely because less academic adolescents have already been eliminated through failure to achieve sufficient success at the 'A' level examinations).

In the second place, personality leads adolescents to choose certain subjects which are in some way geared to their personality. Students of mathematics and philosophy tend to be stable introverts; students of sociology, on the other hand, tend to be unstable extraverts—a fact which will not surprise readers who are familiar with the exploits of sociology students in leading student unrest and militancy. Much detailed knowledge has been built up of these relations between subject matter and personality; these relations appear to be international, in the sense that similar results have been found in different countries.

In the third place, personality interacts with method of teaching in determining ultimate success. Consider the modern 'discovery' method, which is diametrically opposed to the traditional 'exposition' method. The question is sometimes posed: Which of these two methods gives better results? There is no answer to this question—in part because the term 'better' must be closely defined before we can even begin to measure the results of any such study. But assume that we mean here success in acquiring a certain kind of knowledge, together with a liking for the subject; even when objective measurement of the results is possible along these lines, nevertheless the question is still unanswerable. The reason is very simple, and touches on the fundamental weakness of all modern educational dogma. The fire that melts the wax tempers the steel; identical treatment, applied to heterogenous objects (or persons) produces contradictory results. So in the case of educational methods. Discovery methods work with extraverted children, who enjoy the process and do well; it does not work with introverted children (of similar I.Q.), who do not enjoy the process, and do not do well with it. It is impossible to make any general statement about the success or otherwise of these new methods; they work with some, but not with others. Children are not a uniform set of identical twins; they have individuality, and any attempt to treat them all alike, in the hope of achieving uniform results, is doomed to failure.

Many other examples could be given of this universal truth, in the educational field. For example, machine teaching is appreciated more by introverted children, and they tend to do better with it; extraverted children prefer, and do better with, orthodox teaching by teachers. Introverted children are more easily motivated by praise, extraverted ones by blame. Making examinations more stressful improves the performance of stable children, but worsens that of emotionally unstable ones. Even though educational psychologists tend to shy away from the study of individual differences, nevertheless there is sufficient evidence already available to state with considerable certainty that just as children of different intelligence require different approaches, different types of curriculum, and different methods of teaching the academically dull from the academically gifted, so do children of different personality require different approaches, different methods of teaching, and possibly different subject matter. No general decree from on high about any of these matters can obliterate the diversity of human nature, or the fact that a Procrustean bed is not a comfortable one to sleep on—or something to force on our innocent children.

In all discussions of educational matters, from the design of schools to the question of streaming, and of different types of schools versus comprehensive, there seems to be missing this one essential caveat—that there are no universal truths which apply to all children, but that all conclusions apply only to some types of children, and not to others. It seems quite likely that extraverted children like, and do well, in the new 'open' schools, whereas introverted children probably prefer the old-fashioned 'class-room' type of school. (I say 'it seems likely' because there is not sufficient evidence to make this statement any stronger than this.) If this were true it would obviously be quite wrong to make all school building 'open' or traditional; there should be some of one kind and some of the other. This would enable parents (and children) to make intelligent and informed choices, rather than submit to the tyranny of architects and educational authorities.

Procrustes, of course, is the deity of the egalitarians; all must be cut down to the same size, by hook or crook, regardless of the infinite diversity intended by nature. Thus egalitarianism is directly opposed to biological reality, and the educational devices advocated by egalitarians are equally directly opposed to the 'greatest good of the greatest number'—which could only be achieved by allowing children (and their parents) the maximum freedom of choice, in a maximally diversified system of schooling. If different children have different degrees and types of ability, and different personalities geared to different types of teaching, then it makes no sense whatever to insist on complete uniformity; in this way, we do the maximum amount of harm to the largest possible number of children. It will of course never be possible to construct systems of school education which actually optimize the chances of success for each individual child (although the closest possible approach to this goal would seem the most desirable educational ideal), but we can increase individual choice to the maximum possible extent, without increasing financial cost. The facts of human inequality demand different types of education for different children; they demand different aims and different motivations for different children; lastly, they demand different physical structures and different approaches for different children. Human diversity is the one fundamental and obvious fact which is basic to education; genetic research has established beyond any doubt that such diversity as we observe is firmly grounded on biological reality, and is not the result of man-made environmental influences. Equalize the environment as much as we like, we will never reduce human diversity very much from that which we observe today.

An interesting example and proof of this fact is given by work on I.Q. variability in orphanages. Take a group of orphans, taken from their mothers shortly after birth, and all brought up in an orphanage together. Environmental conditions are as similar for the children involved as it is humanly possible to make them—far more so than any government, however egalitarian, could ever succeed in mposing on a whole nation. Under these conditions, did the I.Q. variability of this group of children shrink to nothing? Not at all. There was hardly any shrinkage when these children were compared with outside groups of children exposed to all the inequalities of England during the depression (when this experiment was conducted). In other words, try as we may, we cannot reduce human diversity by anything more than a small and insignificant amount. This is the basic wisdom of biology; education must follow this teaching or it will harm rather than benefit the children who come to be taught, but may stay to curse—as so many of the older, non-academic children are doing nowadays.

Egalitarians sometimes adopt a moral and ethical tone and argue that to treat children differently from each other goes counter to their best interests, and counter to some divine law. Exactly the opposite is the truth. Unless all children are in fact alike in important aspects of their cognitive and emotional nature, to treat them as if they were alike does violence to their biological make-up. Some children delight in academic work, and take to it; others hate academic work, and are unhappy with it. To treat children so contrasting in their attitude and outlook alike does violence to one group or the other—or in fact to both! There is nothing moral or ethical in this approach; nor is it true that the end effect will be to make the two groups of children alike. There is nothing divisive about allowing children to follow their inherited predispositions, and to accept or reject academic ideals as they please; they enter school different from each other in many important ways, and they leave school different from each other in many important ways. Educationalists are realizing more and more that children leave school essentially with what they brought into it; the influence of school in promoting 'equality' is so limited as to be almost non-existent, as Christopher Jencks has pointed out so clearly in his book on *Inequality*, and as Raymond Boudon has demonstrated so clearly in his *Education, Opportunity, and Social Inequality*. There is no moral or ethical justification for trying to do violence to inherited diversity; on the contrary, if we have the good of the children at heart, rather than our own political preconceptions, we shall try to follow their bent and give them the best possible chance to grow up according to their lights. Anything else is tyranny, and intolerable in a democratic society.

It is sometimes argued that 'intelligent children will succeed anyway', even in mixed-ability classes where the teacher's attention is necessarily directed most to the least able; it is also suggested that the good influence of the able on the less able more than makes up for any loss suffered by the more able. There is no evidence for these beliefs, which are adduced merely to shore up the practice of mixing in one class children of very different abilities. On the contrary, the presence of very able children may discourage completely the less able, while the failure of the teacher to let the able children progress at an appropriate rate may (and often does) lead to truancy, disenchantment with school work, and rowdyism. Failure by the teacher at this stage to awaken the enthusiasms of the bright children for academic work may have permanent effects; unfortunately the refusal of 'progressive' educationalists to carry out proper research into the deleterious effects of their egalitarian principles makes it difficult to substantiate

these observations at the level of direct scientific proof.

No doubt the occasional clever child may find his way in spite of the obstacles which egalitarian doctrines put in it; this should not be generalized to apply to all clever children. We can, and do, eat the seed-corn when we fail to give our bright children all the educational support we can. In fact of course we do worse than treat them equally with the average and dull; we give priority to the less able, on the grounds that they are more in need of help. Many teachers actively discourage and hold back the bright children, either intentionally or because not to do so would make teaching a mixed-ability class impossible. The insistence on comprehensive schools, together with the abolition of streaming, goes directly counter to the diversity of ability found in the children forced into this unnatural *Gleichschaltung*; we are already observing the evil consequences, for the bright and the dull alike, of these ideological absurdities. Policies such as these find no support whatever in psychology or genetics; they are derived from political and social ideals which may attract our sympathy but are out of kilter with biological reality.

It is a curious feature of the present situation in education that the majority of those opting for enforced uniformity of schooling for all children are socialists, usually deriving their theories from a Marxist background. Marx himself of course was openly contemptuous of egalitarianism, and one of the main principles of socialism ('From each according to his ability . . .') clearly recognizes individual differences in innate ability. More than that; educational regimes in socialist and communist countries are extremely 'old fashioned' and almost Victorian in their attention to the preservation of order in the classroom, rigid advancement by achievement, and insistence on standards of academic work being maintained. Even more than contemporary America, the U.S.S.R. carefully selects exceptionally able children (particularly in mathematics and physics) and brings them together in specialized institutions directly linked with universities. Even the ban on I.Q. tests, introduced by Stalin when he found in the middle thirties that results did not bear out communist notions of environmental influences, has been lifted. No wonder that the educational standards of countries behind the Iron Curtain are rising while ours are falling; in the 'mathematics olympiads' held annually for schoolchildren, the Iron Curtain countries habitually sweep the board. This is symptomatic of what is happening to educational standards in other subjects too.

We must conclude that in so far as our civilization is based on education, it is in danger of suffering a serious blow through the consistent disregard of biological reality manifested by present-day educational theorists. There are few countries in the world where parents find it more difficult to make decisions about the schooling of their children which will act to the ultimate benefit of these children; their choice is whittled away to vanishing point, and all they are offered are so-called 'modern' comprehensive schools which have abandoned all pretence of teaching traditional subjects along traditional lines, maintaining discipline, and safeguarding academic standards. Such schools may be attractive to some parents and children; they certainly are not so to all parents and children. Human diversity insists on different schools for different children, and on as free and wide-ranging a choice being offered parents and children as is humanly possible.

Ronald Butt

Politics and Education

RONALD BUTT

Of course, education was always in one sense politicized and, in that particular sense, it always must be. Plato and Aristotle were quite clear that, whatever kind of state or society was to be sustained, the young must be educated to its basic values. I do not know of any philosophers since the Greeks who have rejected this assumption, and it goes without saying that in more primitive cultures the upbringing of the young is normally designed to enable the fundamental structure and ethic of the group to be maintained. The Christian Church, of course, always understood this function of education in the centuries of its influence and so have those contemporary secular states which are founded on specific political theories or ideologies—none more so than the anti-religious Communist societies in Russia and China, where the overriding purpose of all education is not simply to produce citizens with the particular skills and aptitudes that the state wants but to condition the future citizen in the total acceptance of the state as it is.

What is more, most political philosophers have understood that if education is to be effective, it must start with the very young: as Aristotle put it, education is the means of making a state into a community and giving it unity—the unity of social customs and mental culture. He also observed that we tend to love the things we know first; quite clearly, it is as possible to train our children to be pickpockets as to train them to be honest, and if we train them to be honest, that alone is to express a judgment about the kind of society in which we wish them to dwell.

Naturally, therefore, education in our modern British state (that is to say, in the period since the state took over the responsibility and duty of seeing that education was provided for every member of the community) has been based on certain implied values. On the whole, until the last decade or so, education in this country has almost wholly proceeded on the assumption that children should grow up to subscribe to the virtues of a Christian, or of a largely Christianity-derived, society. It was assumed that they should be trained in the concepts of good and honourable behaviour that are appropriate to such a society; subscribing to the principles of the authority of lawfulness and tolerance of free ideas under a parliamentary democratic constitution; respecting the political institutions by which this constitution operates and aspiring, as the peak of educational attainment for those able to achieve it, to the high standards of literacy, artistic achievement and scientific understanding that have been the peaks of an evolving but traditional culture.

Within that general consensus, of course, there were differences of opinion about how much education it was feasible or appropriate to provide, given the economic and social circumstances prevailing at any particular time. There were arguments about the number of years to be spent compulsorily in full-time education by those children who were not 'academic' and about the efficacy of one or another sort of channel for educational advancement. Until lately, however, there was no dispute between any of the three major British political parties, or with any substantial section of educational opinion (whatever their differences over the pace and method of advancement) that the basic object of the state's educational activities was to provide equality of opportunity for all children, irrespective of their family background or financial circumstances, and to enable each child to maximize his own potential within a society which had a generally shared concept, however inadequately realized in practice, of what is good education. This approach assumed the desirability of providing the maximum scope (though this was in practice insufficient to enable all the children who might have benefited from it to do so) for those able to profit from what may, for convenience, be called an 'academic' education—in many ways an unsatisfactory description because it may suggest, wrongly, that the goal of all such children ought to be the university.

Now the fact has to be faced straight away that this approach to education implied that the ablest of 'working-class' children would be socialized into the 'middle class'; again, the terminology is unsatisfactory but I use it for want of a better way to describe people who have attained a certain level of literacy, numeracy and self-provision, and who are therefore equipped to pursue certain callings. The renewal and enlargement of the educated middle classes by these means was, until recently, one of the main features of British social life. Sometime in the fifties, however, the consensus that the objective was desirable began to break up. The Labour Party and a rising tide of educational opinion ceased to believe in equality of opportunity in the sense that I have defined it—partly because of its association with a rigid system of selection for different kinds of education which, it is true, sometimes operated unjustly in respect of the late developer. But the deeper reason for the transformation of Labour opinion, and that of 'progressive' educationalists, was their persuasion that the end-product of the old system was inequality of status, and the maintenance of class divisions between the high attainers (irrespective of their family background) and the rest. Equality of opportunity, with the inference that those best able to advance educationally should be provided for appropriately, was rejected in favour of a belief in education as a means of producing a 'classless' society.

It was never exactly clear what was to be implied by 'classless'. How far did it mean the placing of equal value on all kinds of educational capacity and achievement? How far, even, did it imply the emergence of a single style of speech, with a diminished grammar, so that all external differences of origin and of literacy were more or less obliterated? The definition of objectives was imprecise, but it was at least clear that the old equality of opportunity was to a significant extent being replaced by social engineering as the principal criterion by which the educational system was to be judged. Whatever the neighbourhood of a school, whatever the chances, in some cases, that the potential of highly educable children might be diminished by placing them in a school in which they were a small minority, the overriding consideration was that the status of the school should not be diminished by the absence of able children from it. The principle of reverse discrimination was established and, indeed, politicians such as the former Labour Education Secretary, Mr Edward Short, seemed to see education almost entirely in terms of an attempt to rectify the inequalities of nature and social background from the womb onwards.

This change of emphasis was the mainspring of the Labour Party's total commitment to a rapid and ubiquitous movement towards a complete system of comprehensive education, which was assisted by the support of some middle-class people who disliked the old selective system because of the problem it created for their own children if these failed to get into the old grammar schools and were assigned to the secondary modern schools. But, of course, the most rational argument for the new fashion was to be found in the undeniable faults of the old inflexible system of education, which worked badly in respect at least of the 10% who were late developers. This became evidence for the need to switch to comprehensive schools and for building them on a very large scale on the grounds that only size would enable each one to support an element sufficiently academic to lead up to a sixth form, while at the same time placing an equal value and status on all levels of educational achievement. Concepts of class and anti-class and of 'equality' lay at the back of the whole movement. Thus an intelligent fifteen-year-old explained to me recently, in respect of her own school, that it was divided into E, Q, and D blocks in descending educational capacity and that the choice of these letters in preference to A, B, C, was designed to disguise the distinction between the streams 'which we are not supposed to know'.

Although in many areas, particularly where there is a balanced and homogeneous population, the comprehensive school can work well, its establishment in many cases has been associated with problems which are not simply educational in the narrower sense. In many cases, the comprehensive structure has become associated with a 'value-free' approach to teaching which diminishes the regard paid to old academic standards, is anti-examination (or is in favour of examinations that everyone can pass) and, some would even say, is instinctively if not consciously anti-achievement. It is very much concerned with the principle of levelling. There is frequently a stress on the equal value of different 'cultures' and among some teachers a tendency to deride traditional learning as 'middle class'. The fashion of teaching is often based extensively on the pupil's own inclination to 'discover' rather than on teaching him, discipline is free and (symptomatically) children may be encouraged to address their teachers or headmasters by their first names. There is in some city schools endemic disorderly behaviour, a high rate of truancy and a great deal of vandalism, and I believe that this is in part the result of progressive methods. When I discussed some of these problems in an article in *The Times*, mentioning, as an example, the reluctance to discipline children for foul language, a teacher who wrote 'as a young, long-haired tramp who occasionally uses four-letter words in the staff-room of one of Britain's largest comprehensive schools' took issue with me in the correspondence columns in terms that substantially made my case.

'I believe,' he wrote, 'there is as much, probably more good Christianity in this egalitarian, atheistic, progressive, trendy, hard-swearing, free-loving comprehensive than any religious, excellent, patriotic, single-sex, single-caste establishment.' The essential battle of the two cultures in the classroom, and in many cases, between the home and the classroom, could hardly be more clearly stated. In this single statement, the politicizing of education in an entirely new sense—namely that it is now the vehicle used by those who, in varying degrees, wish to change the cultural basis of society—is explicit. This movement is much assisted by a politically motivated segment of the teaching profession whose essential aim is to further this change. In its extreme form, this phenomenon has been demonstrated by the activities of the left-wing teachers' organization 'Rank and File' and by the activities of the National Union of School Students whose propaganda is displayed extensively on so many school notice boards, demanding 'schools not prisons'.

So we see that there has been a rapid transformation of the simple idea of correcting the injustices caused by clumsy forms of selection to a much wider educational concept in which the educational system is to be used as a weapon to change the political system in a manner (even if not for an end) which Plato and Aristotle would have fully appreciated. If this were what the majority of people and particularly parents wanted, then there could be no further argument, but there is no evidence that it is. If this revolutionary goal had been proclaimed in terms as crude as those in which I have stated it, then, of course, there would have been a reaction. But the process has been much more subtle than that and the 'revolutionary' element has been well diluted by the kind of acceptable radicalism which has the power of fashion. It is difficult to overstate the power of a 'going idea' which, once it has the steam of fashion behind it, will harness the opinion-forming establishment of the officials, the academics, the professionals and, not least, the media who will endorse, reflect and magnify it. When an intellectual fashion is at full flood, it ceases to be respectable even to question what is happening for fear of being labelled a reactionary. Criticism becomes a one-way business and those who challenge the fashion are in for a pretty rough ride until, gradually, the fashion overreaches itself and, among ordinary people, it becomes possible to wonder whether, perhaps, it isn't all going too far.

In the making of a climate of fashion, the fact that one political party rather than another is in power is more important than is often supposed. Of course, the process of influence is circular; a party obtains office partly because the climate of informed opinion prepares conditions suitable for it—but once it has arrived, that party has a scope for influencing the norms of the intellectual climate that is easy to underestimate if one judges its success principally in terms of its more concrete intentions, so many of which come unstuck in the face of events. During the six years of the last Labour government, the 'radical' fashion in education gripped not only the reigning politicians and a large part of the teaching profession, but also many local education officers whose influence on local policy is often decisive. The solidification of their convictions about the desirable structure of education, and also about the approach to teaching methods during the years when Labour dominated the intellectual climate, was to be a major obstacle to any subsequent attempts by the Conservatives to move in a different direction. So much was conformity to the prevailing orthodoxy a mark of intellectual and political respectability before 1970 that the Conservative leadership (though not the Conservative rank and file) felt constrained to go along with it to a considerable extent—a process which, one might guess, was made easier for the Conservative leaders precisely because their own children were not generally being educated within the state sector where the revolution in educational attitudes was taking place.

The derision and later the rage which greeted Mrs Thatcher's appointment as Education Secretary in 1970 was symptomatic of what had happened to the climate of educational opinion during the previous six years. Nor was this reaction (faithfully reflected in the educational press) simply the consequence of her politically clumsy decision to save money on school milk as part of the then government's economy drive. The deeper objection to her was that, unlike her predecessor Lord Boyle, she had shown no inclination to swim with the tide and was known to be non-conformist to the orthodoxy which was now firmly entrenched in her own department. It is not unusual for a government department to have its own policy positions in relation to controversial issues but it is not often that they are as politically engaged over issues which are subject to fierce debate between the parties as the D.E.S. had become in the argument over the structure and methods of education. Of course, the D.E.S. was not party political in the narrowest sense, and would have accepted Lord Boyle with some enthusiasm, but the arrival of Mrs Thatcher was met with a certain dismay. Whereas Lord Boyle, in deference to his party's opinion, was prepared to defend the continuance of some selective schools on the grounds of their excellence (for the time being?) Mrs Thatcher had made it clear that she was sceptical about a total switch to a comprehensive system. Lord Boyle seemed prepared to reduce Conservative policy to the familiar one of simply putting a brake on the speed of the inevitable. Mrs Thatcher committed the offence of challenging the concept of inevitability. In 1966, Lord Boyle had indicated that if he became Secretary of State again, he would not straightaway withdraw the Labour departmental circular pressing local authorities to go comprehensive. Mrs Thatcher did immediately withdraw it and what is more, the language in which she talked about education, stressing the need for quality and achievement, accepting a variegated educational structure as good in itself, and believing in a society which rewarded effort and self-reliance, went against the grain of most educationists' ideas. The reception of Mrs Thatcher was distinctly chilly. She was conscious of having to walk warily, and if (for example) she was ever inclined to name someone outside the approved circle for some committee or appointment, she would be told that to do so would be 'provocative'.

In practice, as it turned out, Mrs Thatcher was a good deal more cautious in challenging the orthodoxy than many of her party would have liked. Although, by circular 1070, she restored to local authorities their freedom to propose or not to propose comprehensive schemes, she approved the great majority of such schemes that were submitted to her. She also conformed, apparently with conviction, to the commitment to raise the school-leaving age, despite the misgivings of some in her party about whether this was the best way of spending limited resources. She was cautious in her attitude to direct grant schools, and though she raised more money for them she did not feel powerful enough to reopen the direct grant school list. Her term of office as a whole presented the picture of a Minister ground between the remorseless wheel of an educational establishment which knew what it wanted and the stone of her government colleagues' inertia which arose from the Conservatives' failure to understand the political and social consequences, in the deepest sense, that must inevitably follow if no critique was opposed to the prevailing educational ideology. It was, significantly, not until Mrs Thatcher had turned to the extension of nursery education, which did fit well into this orthodoxy, that she momentarily achieved something like grudging approval, if not popularity, with the educational establishment.

On the other hand, though in a sense little that was tangible was achieved in the three and a half years of Mrs Thatcher's occupancy of the D.E.S., it is probably true to say that (in accordance with the general rule that the ideas of their political masters do wash off to some extent on officials) there was, at the end of it, a greater understanding within the world of educational officialdom that the prevailing attitudes towards teaching and school structure had

not delivered the goods and that some reappraisal was necessary. There was concern about rising illiteracy; it ceased to be wholly disreputable to challenge 'do-as-you-like' teaching methods; the public's concern about the indiscipline of many schools and their children's learning failure was manifest; in London parents were keeping children out of school when they were unwilling to accept schools not of their own choice; the idea that the parents should begin to have more say, somehow, in what was happening in the schools was taken on board. It is difficult to quantify how far attitudes within the educational establishment had genuinely changed but it was at least understood that there was now a case that had to be answered and not simply derided.

There are, however, few signs of any fundamental change of attitudes. In the case of school structure, for example, the escape route from the present dilemma seems for many educationalists to lie in the argument that if there is a specific problem arising from comprehensive schools, it is associated with size (which begs as many questions as it answers). On the whole, the endeavour is simply to find answers to the challengers which do not in any substantial way alter the basis of received doctrine. The fundamental problem remains that there is very little accountability between the educational processes and the general public, either directly or through the politicians. The Secretary of State has, of course, no control over curricula. (One significant aspect of this is that it permits the teaching of a new morality under the guise of social and sex teaching in many schools—where, in the urge to teach about contraception, assumptions are made about the likely moral behaviour of children which may be self-fulfilling. Yet there is usually little or no consultation with parents, and the Secretary of State is powerless to intervene.) Nor does he or she have the same control over standards of teaching since the old formal system of school inspection by ministry inspectors was abolished. No doubt it could not be restored in its old form for fear of teachers' hostility; yet surely some better means of national inspection and scrutiny than now is possible by the 500 or so inspectors at the Secretary of State's disposal would help. It no longer seems sensible to leave this so extensively to the eccentricities of some local educational authorities who are often dominated by their own officials; what is needed is some greater accountability to parents and to the public in the light of criteria publicly established in Whitehall, and with Parliament taking a greater interest about what happens to the public funds it supplies for education.

Meanwhile, the polarization of educational opinion between what can roughly, for shorthand purposes, be called 'left' and 'right' continues—with the left having the monopoly in the places of power, and the right having, in the last analysis, a great deal of inchoate public support and disquiet on which it can draw. Of course, the politicization of education that has been so important is a subtle business; it would be crude and quite inaccurate to suppose that everyone who has been involved in the fashionable view wishes fundamentally to change the values of society in some anarchical direction. Nevertheless there is a spectrum of opinion supporting broadly the same educational process which, at one end, wishes to do this (no doubt for the idealistic reasons which have always animated those who are prepared to see liberty spill over into licence) and which (much more powerfully) at the other simply sees what is happening as the right way of achieving a fair and more egalitarian society. It is the extent to which the same umbrella covers such disparate interests that constitutes the danger. If anyone should suppose that I have caricatured the motives of the social and political engineers in parliament, he should refer to either the Labour Party's

'Green Paper' programme of June 1973 or to the speeches of Mr Edward Short when Education Minister. Labour's Green Paper was quite explicit. 'The traditional definition of equality of opportunity in education has not proved, by itself, an adequate basis to meet the varying needs of people or to compensate for the social factors which limit the ability of the majority to take advantage of opportunities offered. . . . Democratization . . . must be a major theme of education reform in the 70s. . . . It also means positive discrimination in the application of resources . . . in favour of people who are disadvantaged for social, economic, environmental, sex or physical reasons.'

Much of this positive discrimination makes use of teaching attitudes which cannot be said to add to the literacy of those to whom it is supposed to be directed but which, if anything, often seem to have the reverse effect. Even more seriously, its impact on the standards of education more generally is such that the question arises—what will be the consequences for the able and

the willing of whatever background? In the process of 'reverse discrimination', what penalties are to be imposed on other abler children, from a perhaps equally disadvantaged background, and with what consequences? What social values are to be inculcated in schools, regardless of the wishes of the community? What is to be the limit with social engineering? We need not dispute that all education is, as I said at the beginning, politicized. We are entitled to ask whether it should be politicized anew by the will of a freemasonry of experts and social engineers whose ideas and practices have never been adequately tested by any political or democratic processes—precisely because education is so largely in the hands of non-responsive officials or experts, or is under the control of local politicians who are generally elected on completely other grounds than educational policy. The objection is not to the politicization of education but to the non-accountable and non-representative form that the present politicization is taking.

Can the Universities Survive?

MAX BELOFF

By putting the question in so stark a fashion I clearly do not mean to suggest that in the near, or even the more distant, future we shall see no institutions anywhere in the world that call themselves universities. It is a commonplace that the names of institutions may continue to exist while their function and organization are profoundly altered. Hobbes saw this when he spoke of the Holy Roman Empire as being the ghost of the Roman Empire sitting crowned on the grave thereof; and the Holy Roman Empire itself as it existed when Napoleon put an end to it was very unlike what Charlemagne or the Ottonians were trying to create or re-create. Indeed, I would go further and suggest that sometimes the struggle to keep the name of an institution alive may actually damage the goals that the institution is meant to promote. In other words, we may well go on having universities, perhaps have more and more of them, and larger and larger ones, and yet lose sight altogether of the main purposes for which they exist.

The second point that I want to stress is that I am of necessity writing mainly about universities in what may broadly be called the Western world: Western Europe, the United States, Australasia. Not that universities are confined to these areas—far from it; hardly a state is so poor that does not offer at least one university—like a national airline, it is a symbol of having arrived. But it seems clear that all universities have in fact been developed out of the original European models, either through their implantation by colonization or imperial authority, or by voluntary imitation. Even countries with sophisticated civilizations of their own have as far as I know no universities that claim antecedents prior to their contacts with Europe or North America—although education and scholarship, the preservation and transmission of knowledge were of course promoted in other ways.

In the third place, I am all too well aware that, even before the massive developments and changes of the last quarter-century, there existed very considerable difference of opinion as to the essence of a university both between different countries and even within them. For instance, when Newman wrote his *Idea of a University* in 1852, he defined a university as 'a place of teaching universal knowledge'.[1] And the emphasis on teaching and on a liberal rather than a vocational approach to the curriculum underlies his entire argument:

The process of training, by which the intellect instead of being formed or sacrificed to some particular or accidental purpose, to some specific trade or profession, or study or science, is disciplined for its own sake, for the perception of its own proper object and for its own highest culture, is called Liberal Education; and although there is no-one in whom it is carried as far as is conceivable, or whose intellect would be a pattern of what intellects should be made, yet there is scarcely anyone but may gain an idea of what real training is, and at least look towards it, and make its true scope and result, not something else his standard of excellence; and numbers there are who may submit themselves to it, and secure it to themselves in good measure. And to set forth the right standard, and to train according to it, and to help forward all students towards it, according to their various capacities, this I conceive to be the business of a University.[2]

And the practical end—and there must always be a practical end in anything to which the community is asked

[1] John Henry, Cardinal Newman, *The Idea of a University* (edition of 1886). Preface p. 1.
[2] Ibid. pp. 152–3.

45

to devote resources—is that of 'training good members of society'.[3] Thus Newman regarded the passing on of knowledge and the training of minds as much more important for a university than adding to the sum of knowledge available by scholarly inquiry or scientific research. Indeed he praised the division found in a number of European countries between the tasks of the university and the tasks of the different academies: 'to discover and to teach are distinct functions; they are also distinct gifts and not commonly found united in the same person. He who spends his day in dispensing his existing knowledge to all comers is unlikely to have either leisure or energy to acquire new.'[4]

Until relatively recently English universities although giving greater scope than Newman to scholarship and research were on the whole inspired by the kind of ideas to which he gave voice. But elsewhere, under the influence largely of the German model, the distinction between teaching and research was to a great extent eroded. The professor was expected to stand at the very frontiers of knowledge and to guide his students towards them. Nevertheless the distinction between the university and the academy in Newman's sense is not to be overlooked. And in one major country in our time—Soviet Russia—the tasks of higher education and research are divided precisely in this way; nor, as I shall argue, can we be certain that we shall not need in the West to look much more closely at this possible solution to some of our problems.

In 1930, when Abraham Flexner published his once much-read *Universities: American, English, German*, the influence of the German model, somewhat transmuted in the United States, was probably at its height. For Flexner, the British universities—Oxford and Cambridge especially but not by any means solely—were in danger of being demoted from the ranks of the great universities of the world by their adherence to the primacy of undergraduate teaching which he found hard to distinguish in principle from secondary education; and of course the transition from a good 'sixth form' to an Oxford or Cambridge college was at that time one very easy to make. For Flexner, a university consisted of students at both the undergraduate and the graduate level, but it was the graduate school that was in his own phrase 'the heart of the University'.[5]

Flexner's terminology is of course much affected by the fact that his frame of reference was American and his own special field of interest, medicine; but broadly speaking the distinction in emphasis was indeed there at the time. From the point of view of today's Oxford and Cambridge, the striking fact is how rapidly they have moved, at least in numerical terms, towards the Flexner ideal. Oxford in 1930, out of just over 5,000 students in residence, had 212 reading for advanced degrees: about 4%. In 1973, in a university just about twice the size in numbers of students, there were 3,149 working for advanced degrees—over 28%.

Bearing in mind this development, and parallel developments elsewhere in the western world, we would I think now say that what we mean by a university is a place where higher education of both a general and a vocational kind goes on within a context in which research and training for research are also of the essence. The balance may vary, but both elements must be present. But to say this is not enough; if it were, my original question would seem absurd. The world is studded with institutions which claim to be doing just what we have described.

What other conditions would we think a university must fulfil? The most obvious one is that it must not only be free

to embark upon any area of subject-matter that seems relevant to its purpose but also free to follow the argument where it leads. We would have very serious reservations about a university which reserved a certain area of subject-matter as settled once and for all in terms of a religious or secular faith or ideology. We would be even more doubtful of the claims of a university all of whose staff or students or both had to be avowed adherents of a particular creed or philosophy, although such reservations would still have been rejected by most people in this country in the first half of the nineteenth century and are today rejected in the countries of the Communist world.

No-one not himself the adherent of a totalitarian creed who thinks about universities in the light of their history is likely to minimize the importance of some insulation from politics; Flexner looking at the American State Universities was conscious of this danger, but believed that in Europe respect for learning and a conviction of the utility of science would prove a sufficient safeguard. 'The political upheavals which occur in American Universities are beyond imagining in Germany.'[6] Written less than three years before Hitler's assumption of power, the irony is painful indeed.

For England, which Flexner did not credit with much respect for either learning or scientific endeavour, another safeguard existed against undue political interference, the extent to which the education system as a whole was a product of voluntary effort and privately supported: 'Aversion to state interference, not to say state control, is still powerful and effective in England. Hence, a state monopoly of education was and is unthinkable.'[7] Written during the lifetime of the second Labour government this remark also is not without its irony for a reader living under the fourth.[8]

What was envisaged as possible even in western countries, at least in theory, was then that outside pressures would limit the freedom of universities. Political or religious fanaticism would become a menace; dependent as universities everywhere had become or were becoming on the public purse, the point of entry was easy enough to find. What Flexner did not consider possible, in an advanced country at any rate—and his field of observation was limited—was that universities themselves would wish to or even be willing to qualify freedom of speech or inquiry, that students themselves might use violence or the threat of violence to silence those with whom they disagreed, still less that in so using their physical strength they would find defenders among the university faculty itself. The Nazi era was to show how important an element in the immediate situation was overlooked by Flexner; and events in the United States, in Britain and throughout Western Europe in the last decade have made it impossible to look at the Germany of the 1930s and go on saying complacently 'it cannot happen here'. Nor is the scale of such activity the crucial issue; the crucial issue for the survival of universities is whether they themselves and all who work in or for them subscribe to the idea of a university of which freedom of teaching and research is a cardinal element.

But while Flexner was somewhat over-optimistic about this aspect of the future of universities, he was fully alive to a much more difficult and ambiguous aspect of their relationship to society at large; and it was here that his Ameri-

[3] Ibid. p. 177.
[4] Ibid. Preface p. xiii.
[5] Abraham Flexner, *Universities: American, English, German*. O.U.P. 1930, p. 263.

[6] Flexner, op. cit. p. 348 fn.
[7] Ibid. p. 225.
[8] The hostility shown by some members of the Council for National Academic Awards to the idea of academic innovation by a private institution, the University College at Buckingham, shows the inroads that statism and egalitarianism have made in this country.

can background gave his remarks their particular force. Can service to society produce demands on the universities which end by denaturing them in the sense of subordinating what they alone can do to functions which however harmless or even benign are not really for them?

With the experience of American universities in mind, Flexner's main concern was with their extensions of the curriculum to subjects which, however useful, were not sufficiently demanding intellectually to deserve recognition by a university: 'Practical importance is not a sufficient title to academic recognition: if that is the best that can be said, it is an excellent reason for exclusion. A university is therefore not a dumping ground. Universities that are held to their appropriate tasks will be unfit to do any other.' [9] It was not, he argued, that born scholars and scientists would not find their way to good work even in a system which lacked general respect for intellectual standards; it is however, he wrote, a 'question whether the term "university" can be saved or is even worth saving'.[10] In other words what Flexner called the university as a 'public service institution' or what is now in this country referred to as a 'comprehensive university' is to be regarded as something which by its nature cannot fulfil the prime function of a university proper.[11]

It must I think be clear that Flexner's argument while very understandable in the light of American experience was not quite as self-evident as he thought. To insist on a hierarchy of subjects is one thing: 'practical poultry-raising' was a less suitable component of a Columbia degree course than say, philosophy. But to make lack of relevance to practice the test was curious for someone whose main interest was in clinical medicine. To regard universities as unconcerned with the society around them is as extreme a point of view as to reduce them to a merely vocational role. The more the history of universities is studied, the more it is clear how important has been their response to changing social conditions. Their shift in the country from narrowly ecclesiastical concerns to a wider function in respect of training the élites of a largely secular society has been studied profitably and in depth by Dr Mark Curtis;[12] and no doubt when the volumes of the projected History of Oxford University appear from the press we shall know even more about this and other periods. Nor can Newman's vision be dismissed so lightly as Flexner with his strong bias in favour of the German model would seem to do. It is true that if one despairs of the standards of secondary education (as Flexner was inclined to) one would see undergraduate education as making up for its deficiencies rather than as higher education in the full sense; but undergraduate education and secondary education can be, and surely should be, distinguishable. And Flexner, thinking too much of Arnold (Thomas not Matthew), was inclined to overestimate the character-building side and underestimate the intellectual tradition of the best English schools; as a pupil in one of them at the time when Flexner was lecturing, I think I can testify on that point.

What is true is that a university which expands by the dilution of its intellectual concerns is likely to make these seem less important, and above all to blunt the edge of discrimination, so that the value attached to a degree however obtained is thought of as a constant. But the important thing here is not as Flexner seems to imply what is thought

by the administration or the teaching body but by the students themselves. For if we turn from the way things looked in America and to an American in 1930, to the here and now in Britain, I think that one could say that the most obvious change is in the attitude of the student body, or rather of a part of it, to the claims made for science and learning. It is not that the undergraduate body in the ancient British universities in the 1930s was wholly composed of dedicated scholars, but that those who did no more than the bare minimum of work necessary to avoid being sent down and for the rest of the time pursued other interests proper to healthy young men—or even some improper ones—did not themselves deny in principle the value of the studies they saw going on around them. They might, if inflamed by drink, mildly persecute a too-obviously superior young intellectual, but they would not have thought of acting in concert to disrupt the studies of their contemporaries in pursuit of some ideological objective of their own—and if they had done they would have expected to suffer an appropriate penalty. But Flexner was wrong in believing that a decline in standards would come about solely or even mainly through the dilution of content; Oxford has not offered even for the B.Ed., as did the celebrated Columbia Teachers' College in his time, courses in 'cookery-fundamental processes', 'fundamental problems in clothing', 'family meals', 'principles of home laundering' and so on. The source of our troubles lies not in the intrusion of the practical but in the perversion of the truly academic.

It is true that this may not be the end of the story. If the idea of the 'comprehensive university' does come to dominate educational policy in this country, then the pressure for parity of esteem between institutions might become within multi-purpose institutions pressure for parity of esteem between subjects. If this were confined to verbal genuflections in this direction, it might not matter much—who loses if we have professors of cooking or laundering or whatever? But if it is translated into financial terms, if great libraries or major laboratories have to accept formulae for grants based on the needs of purely vocational subjects the ultimate result could be disastrous . . . and the prospect is not all that far-fetched. The combination of philistinism and egalitarianism which one finds in some discussions of such things as the Arts Council, or the British Council and to which the B.B.C. itself now bows from time to time is an augury of what to expect.

But, as I have said, this is not so deep-seated a weakness as that which arises from misconceptions more directly related to the university's performance in what has hitherto been regarded as its proper sphere. That problem has many facets. They are not always easy to distinguish.

In the first place, there is the extension to higher education of the belief that is almost an orthodoxy in respect of schooling, namely that individuals should not be selected on the basis of their ability to study particular branches of knowledge in particular types of institutions, that it is on the contrary possible to eliminate selection, and to modify the content of courses and the nature of the institutions to suit any and every student who may come along however random his commitment. So far the advocates of this interpretation of the egalitarian creed have been so preoccupied with their attack on traditional patterns in secondary education that they have not devoted much attention to the universities. But there is something in the view that in all these matters what Britain does tends belatedly to follow what the United States has pioneered, and there we have already seen this doctrine in operation, notably in the 'open admissions' systems as practised for instance in New York. The results are what might be expected, but since the pressure for such a system is

[9] Flexner, op. cit. p. 27.
[10] Ibid. p. 213.
[11] For a defence of 'comprehensive higher education' see, for example, the article by Christopher Price, 'Levelling down the élite pyramid', *Times Higher Education Supplement*, 1 June 1973.
[12] Mark H. Curtis, *Oxford and Cambridge in Transition, 1558–1642*. Oxford, 1959.

political not educational, the evidence of academic results will not necessarily convince its sponsors.

Under the same heading comes what is usually called positive discrimination—which means making the universities carry the burden of real or alleged injustices to particular groups in the population in respect of their own social, educational and cultural position.[13] The most obvious case is the admission of students to universities irrespective of their fitness provided they are members of such groups. In the case of the Black Americans, this has been camouflaged to some extent by the creation of departments of so-called Black Studies, which being in the end a way of deceiving the intended beneficiaries of positive discrimination are likely to create even more bitterness than existed in the situation the measures were designed to correct. An even heavier burden is placed upon all universities by the demand to give preference in making appointments to blacks, women and so forth. In other words, the universities must either adopt a quota system— a *numerus clausus*—or go to great lengths positively to prove that, say, a vacant chair of aerodynamics cannot be filled—except at great risk to future aviators—by a black Spanish-speaking woman who happens to profess the Jewish religion. Once again, particularly in a rich country like the United States, these things can be managed. The whole business of recruitment of staff can be done in so elaborate a way that the necessary proof of a willingness to comply with the law can be furnished; persons appointed to meet a quota can be shunted off into some relatively harmless academic byway. But in countries like Britain, where total resources are very tightly limited, positive discrimination could wreak havoc.

It will be seen that these are instances where politics intervenes through law-making bodies to impose norms that the universities would not of their own inclination ever wish to adopt. The same is true of university government. The recruitment of students to the governing bodies of universities is something which has been imposed by politicians—with major effect in Germany and Denmark, to a lesser extent so far by the authorities in this country. In Germany, the system of *drittelparitaet*—meaning one-third academics, one-third students and one-third non-academic staff on all university bodies—has meant the politicization of universities in respect of appointments— and the watering down of curricula and standards. In Denmark it has led to an almost total domination of universities by the organized and violent left-wing minority of the student body. Once again, the state has imposed upon the universities something they would not have done if free to choose.

And that brings one to a cardinal question—why should one oppose association of students with governance of universities—a revival of the 'student universities' of the early Middle Ages as against the 'master universities' which came to be the norm, a reversal of fortunes between Bologna and Paris?[14] The reason must surely lie in the quite different concept that has been developed since the Middle Ages of the nature of the learning that universities exist to impart. If one assumes that there is a finite body of knowledge which students require to learn so as to exercise a profession, then there is no reason in principle why they should not get together to hire professors just as a group of would-be footballers might hire a coach to teach them the game. But we do not now think of knowledge as finite, nor

of its acquisition as merely a qualification for a particular career. Only those who are of the academic community and have been involved in it for some time can make valid judgments as to the appropriateness of curricula, the ways in which teaching should be organized and the qualities of those best fitted both to teach and to advance their subject. The medical profession wisely provides that an approach to a specialist doctor should be through a general practitioner, on the grounds that the patient cannot know except by chance what kind of specialist he needs, still less who would be the right man. To say that students can take a serious part in running academic affairs is to suggest that they are somehow born with the knowledge and understanding which it is the purpose of their coming to the university to acquire.

A particular feature of student intervention in academic matters is to be found at present in the field of examinations. It is I think not accidental that examination of some kind has been a central feature of the university scene from the earliest times. The right to confer degrees is the principal right that distinguishes a university from other institutions —though the nomenclature may be blurred as in the case of the Liberal Arts Colleges in the United States. A degree is a sign that the holder has satisfied some objective test of his competence. The award of 'classes' is intended to help his future employers and others to have reasonably correct expectations about his performance. If every student got a degree or if every mark were 100% such discrimination would be impossible, and the teaching aspect of the university reduced to a sham. Methods of examination have of course varied a great deal through the centuries, and do necessarily vary as between different disciplines. But whenever they have been taken seriously they have had in common a determination to avoid as far as possible reliance on interested parties, the student's own teachers, for instance, and some guarantees against a falsification of performance.

Against this view must be set that of some students who have not lacked encouragement in higher quarters that all this is unnecessary, and that objective tests are both artificial and a psychological strain to which the sensitive young should not be exposed. Seeing a degree only as a bread-ticket and claiming it as of right, they cannot see why any student should not be entitled to one; therefore they demand 'continuous assessment', the allotment of long periods of time with full access to libraries and other forms of assistance in dealing with such examination papers as are set, and so forth. If any students fail to make the grade, however defined, they reserve the right to use pressure of various kinds to reverse the verdict. What used to be thought of as peculiar to countries outside Europe that had adopted the notion of the 'university' without understanding it, is now a commonplace in Germany, Italy, Scandinavia and Britain. When the authorities of the University of York overruled in a matter of examination failures the entire Department of Economics of their own university they struck a blow against the whole idea of the university far more serious than they seem to have realized.[15]

Another and quite different threat to universities has, as I have observed already, emerged as the result of the same combination of manipulated student opinion and the pusillanimity of the university itself. And that of course is

[13] See Professor Richard A. Lester's report to the Carnegie Commission on Higher Education summarized by Frances Hill in the *T.H.E.S.*, 9 August 1974.

[14] I follow the distinction adumbrated in Hastings Rashdall, *The Universities of Europe in the Middle Ages*, ed. F. M. Powicke and A. B. Emden. Vol. I, Oxford, 1936.

[15] It is not my intention to single out the University of York in this context. A recent very bad case occurred at Oxford where a student who failed to turn in any answers at all on two of the papers set (out of eight) was allowed a degree on the basis of an improvised oral examination in the subjects concerned. No medical or other reasons were offered by the candidate for his failure to write the original two papers. If Oxford behaves in this way what can one expect elsewhere?

the threat to academic freedom. Here we cannot maintain that the concept itself as it has come to be understood today is of very great age. For most of their history universities were, as I have said, bound by the canons of theological orthodoxy; some subjects could not be inquired into beyond a certain point lest they cast doubt upon revealed religion; and religious tests were imposed upon teachers and taught. But although we have in the world denominational universities which are to some extent limited to the faithful, most people a generation ago would have agreed that it was part of a university's business to encourage research even in directions where the results might be uncomfortable, and to allow the proponents of unusual views full freedom to expound them. The indignation of the world of learning was visited upon Nazi Germany when every canon of academic freedom (as well as other kinds of freedom) was violated by the actions of German universities in response to political pressure from the Party and the State.

Now the same threat to academic freedom has emerged again in Germany itself, though the source of the threat is on the political left and not on the right. But it is not in Germany alone that student groups have assumed the right to make it impossible for views of which they disapprove to get a hearing. Let me be quite clear what I mean. I am not thinking of the attacks upon political figures whose speaking engagements happen to be in universities. It would be difficult to insist that universities should be compelled to provide an arena for their propaganda, and the extent to which this should be done is a matter of general civil liberties, not of academic freedom. I mean quite specifically the alleged right of students to prevent a hearing being given to accredited members of the academic community either because the conclusions of their researches may be unpalatable, or because in matters other than those in which they are academically engaged they have attracted unfavourable attention.

We look back at the age of Galileo and wonder that men should have tried to prevent progress in our understanding of the physical universe; yet to know whether or not the races of man are different in their natural endowment or what are the respective components of nature and nurture in educational achievement is even more important than to know whether the earth goes round the sun or vice versa. Nor can one follow the extraordinary argument put forward by a leading figure in the *soi-disant* Council for Academic Freedom and Democracy that academic freedom is not violated if the victim happens to be a member of another university and not of the staff of the university where the violation takes place: 'The denial of freedom of speech to someone who does not teach in the particular institution concerned, whether that denial is justified or not, cannot be described as a denial of academic freedom.'[16] In other words it would be wrong to stop Professor Eysenck from lecturing in the University of London—though that has been done—but all right to beat him up at Leeds. We may feel that the age of the wandering scholar has passed, but a denial from within the academic community that universities are part of a national and international fraternity of science and learning, and that scholars at one university owe attention or courtesy to those at another, is the kind of revelation that ranks as a glimpse into the abyss.

A peculiar distinction of this kind would of course enable its adherents to justify the notorious failure of the University of Sussex in 1973 to provide a hearing for its duly invited academic guest, Professor Samuel Huntington of Harvard. In this case, it was not the presumed contents of Professor Huntington's undelivered lectures but allegations about his views on the Vietnam war and his service with his own government that were the pretexts for the action taken. As usual the actual work of disrupting the lecture was done by students. But they were publicly supported after the event by seventeen members of staff. The fact that persons who are in principle hostile to academic freedom are allowed to remain on the faculty of a university is yet another sign of the extent to which the desire to avoid physical confrontation with student minorities can descend into an acceptance of intellectual and moral positions which gives away the whole case for universities existing at all.

One is oppressed by the fatalism with which the idea that student violence must be expected unless student demands are agreed to, and that discipline cannot be imposed without wrecking the university, has come to prevail in the West. Lord Annan's report on the University of Essex makes sad reading in this respect as do many of the comments made upon it. The Soviet Union regards discipline in the traditional sense as a necessary part of learning at any level, and seems to find no difficulty in getting this attitude accepted, and students themselves to participate in enforcing it. The fact that the university student costs the community so much money to educate is rightly seen by Soviet academics as a good reason for limiting access to the qualified, and for getting rid of those students who cannot stand the academic pace.[17]

When therefore one asks 'Can the universities survive?' it is clear that one's answer must depend upon one's assessment of the extent to which the modern university and the society that it serves can find a basis for co-existence and mutual support. The omens are deeply unfavourable. The university is of necessity imbued with a set of values to which modern democratic societies are either hostile or indifferent. The university is necessarily hierarchical, society democratic; the university must continually select, society is largely pledged to egalitarianism; the university demands clarity of thought, democratic societies rest upon equivocation. Since society as represented by governments responsible to mass electorates has the upper hand, the university's capacity for resistance is weak. The fact that universities need increasing resources to carry on their work makes for an even greater degree of vulnerability; each addition to their budgets limits their freedom of action.

In such circumstances the belief that the universities can survive by continuous retreat and by a series of judicious compromises seems very implausible. Their only real chance is to convert society to their own view of what is needed. And this in turn means a reversal of their recent tactics, at any rate in this country. Instead of apologizing for their own existence and privileges and attempting to meet their critics half-way, they need leaders who will be absolutely intransigent about fundamentals whether the challenge comes from the politicians, from their own students, or from the traitors in their midst. It would be far better for a university to close down altogether (or be closed down) rather than admit a lowering of its standards through accepting the bypassing of its examination system, or a concession to the enemies of academic freedom by failing to give proper protection to an invited lecturer or to its own staff. The University can survive the loss of some universities—it cannot survive a large-scale

[16] Ralph Miliband, 'Is disruption on the campus ever justified?' *T.H.E.S.*, 10 May 1974.

[17] The position was clearly stated in an interview given by the Soviet professor of political science, Michael S. Woslenski, and published in the German newspaper *Die Zeit* on 19 April 1974, at the end of his stay as a visiting professor at the University of Münster.

defection from the ideas that are essential to its purpose.[18]

Such a line of thought can lead in two directions. One could envisage an attempt to retain the University as both a teaching and a research institution but on a reduced scale, rather as France has retained the standards of the *grandes écoles* by sacrificing its universities to the 'reformers'. Would society accept this minimum concession to élitism as it would be styled if it could have its own way with most of the higher education system? Alternatively, as I hinted earlier, one could look at Newman's ideas or to the Soviet model according to ideological taste and separate the instruction of students from the pursuit of knowledge.

[18] When the original version of this paper was discussed at a meeting of the Carlyle Club it was pointed out by a distinguished politician that while the cure for nonsense was the closure of the institution concerned, such vested interests built up in any university, however new, that it was practically impossible for the Government to contemplate closure despite its control over the purse-strings. So we may expect Essex to survive.

Academies physically separated from Universities, un-affected by the gusts of student politics, could perform their allotted tasks; and society in the end would benefit by their labours.[19] The transformation of a system such as ours into one of this kind raises obvious practical difficulties but it is not theoretically an absurdity. It may be easier for a democratic society to accept this model than a distinction between different levels of University. On the other hand, while it might solve society's problems in respect of the promotion and diffusion of science, it would do so at the expense of the University as we have known it. Euthanasia may be a gentle kind of death but it is death all the same.[20]

[19] Similar ideas in respect of the threat to American universities have been suggested by the distinguished diplomat and historian, George Kennan.

[20] I should perhaps add that we hope at Buckingham to show that the traditional model can still be given a new lease of life if careful thought is given to the problems it is likely to face. Although it will begin on Newman rather than on Flexner lines we certainly envisage research as well as teaching as an integral part of our activities.

The American University: the Anatomy of Current Peace

DEREK COLVILLE

Britain's universities, lagging slightly behind America, are still suffering the disturbance of fragmentary demos and sit-ins; in America now there is peace. It is an atmosphere in which I spend my professional career, and since much of it is doubtless ready for export, the current peace of the American university may be worth closer examination.

Certain features stand out, and I do not think an observer of any political or educational persuasion could convincingly deny them. Qualifications apply: I speak of a large state university of good reputation; details and proportions change somewhat in the private university, but not much, and enough of the implications concern western universities generally, and certainly Britain's.

First, it is fair to say there have been benefits from the outbursts of the late sixties. One has been quite direct: though the actual government of the campus I speak of has returned to a faculty senate, students now sit on many committees. They supply student opinion, and since they are mostly bright radicals who still—for reasons which follow—find politics the most real thing the university can give them, they are serious, informed and, nowadays, careful. These things more than compensate for naïveté, and they do not feel the boredom, or indulge in the consequent committee game-playing, of the faculty. The other benefits of the revolution are mostly unintentional, sometimes ironically so; for instance the double standards set up to encourage open admissions, while still unprotested by most members of staff, have largely been seen through by the minorities they were intended to benefit, who indignantly now ask to confront genuine and not spurious tests. A good example is the demise of Black Studies; a better, perhaps, is that of Black English. It was the fashion in the sixties for white radicals to assure blacks (usually in standard American) that the argot of the ghetto was as effective, respectable and beautiful as any language, and was to be cultivated as their own proud heritage. Since the objects of this shattering condescension are not fools, it has

not taken long for them to ridicule it. William Raspberry, a black columnist, responds with the dry suggestion that since we are to accept the normal speaking, reading and addition of a ghetto child as valid, he can be given all A's on, or before, his arrival at school; the money saved on school buildings, adds Mr Raspberry, could be spent on useful unemployment and welfare payments.

A further fruit of the sixties university rebellion is the reward falling into the laps of those faculties who spoke out against its more spectacular excesses, in defence of academic standards. They are now left severely alone, pariahs free from both election and appointment, and thus largely exempt from endless committee work, they are left to think, teach and write. It may be an incidental reward, but it is pleasant, hard earned, and exclusive.

But these are small matters; a broader look at the elements composing the university is more ominous. The economic shadow, of course, falls over student life. There is a fierce struggle for the public mind, between politician and educational administrator, over the subsidy of higher education. Politicians threaten that students shall pay a more realistic share of the cost: students, and university presidents, resist. There is in fact a shortage of students at many private colleges and universities, and a fairly new phenomenon is the private college ('a happy, self-fulfilling place') advertising for students on television. There is also a desperate shortage of jobs, for the new Ph.D. Under-graduates are deeply career-oriented, and often compete passionately for grades. To do them justice, though, even five years ago, given the option of 'no élitism, no grades, no failures', an overwhelming majority—perhaps for practical reasons, perhaps not—chose to go on having its work formally evaluated.

The academic life of students is confused. The curriculum, in the sense of a considered set of structured degree requirements, has been destroyed, a casualty of 'do-your-own-thing', and all but the brightest and most dedicated appear lost. A vague Rousseauesque fragment persists as undergraduate faith: somehow, if only the right changes could be made, the university could issue the perfectly realized life to every individual. Responsibility for the cost of this naïve romantic fable belongs less to the undergraduate than to the university itself. By its failure to insist that its primary role is the cultivation of thought, by which the individual helps himself, and by its flirtation with the role of social reformer, it has seemed to offer a Utopia it cannot provide. Thus confused students find a home in large lecture courses with superficial social and topical appeal: ultra-recent history, World War II, Nazi Germany, Contemporary Problems (with many films), post-modern literature, futurism, and so on. And Relevance still triumphs. This, again, is an economic as well as academic (or rather anti-academic) matter. Mass lecture courses of superficially popular appeal (e.g. *The Detective Story* in English departments) with large enrolments and one teacher, have become the economic means by which smaller, traditionally academic courses can be maintained. It is a marvellously clear example—to anticipate one major conclusion of this essay—of the inevitable result of combining higher-education-for-nearly-all with the elective course system.

Within the more traditional courses a familiar American phenomenon has become more pronounced: a line, now rather a chasm, exists between those seriously involved with the material, and those who wish only mild trouble-free entertainment, and to glide by with a minimum of work to a vaguely passable B.A. The proportions are roughly one-third to two-thirds, and this too goes back a long way; it is the gulf of difference which has grown recently. It is an important development, of which I shall remind the reader in a later context.

A university, essentially, is its staff, and it is fairly easy to summarize the situation of staff at present. Here again a surface peace obscures a most crucial loss, again a casualty of the sixties. It is simply that the staple of a university, a climate of living, involved, intellectual discussion, no longer exists. There is, in the best sense of an abused term, no dialogue, but only the sterile avoidance of issues, and a resentful inertia varying in tone from weariness to cynicism. It is not hard to explain this, if one considers the various faculty factions during the disrupted years. No single element can now be content with the legacy it has. The few who defended academic values in the sixties have done no better than see the trauma pass; certainly they have seen no return to the values they defended. For the similarly few active and radical members of the staff who, as one student recently put it, 'like to think of themselves as liberals . . . who . . . know what issues ought to concern students but also precisely what their views on such issues should be'—for those, the passing of the riotous years has brought not only the frustrations of anti-climax, but often the loss of what had suddenly promised to be new and influential phases in their careers. But for the rest—by far the largest proportion of staff—who simply sat out the sixties troubles, waiting to discern the probable winner, there has been none to discern. There has been no clear-cut victory to which to attach themselves finally, and they are left in much the same sort of suspension as most undergraduates.

In some ways the third major figure in the university, the professional administrator, has been the most fortunate in what the sixties have left him. The impulse which, in Britain in the late fifties, set up the U.S.-style administrative tower as the vital (as well as physical) centre of the new university has, in reaction to the stresses of disruption, prospered to fantastic levels of growth and complexity, and the result is that administrators are both in demand and frenetically occupied. The sixties troubles posed large problems, and problems, even where pointless or insoluble, generate inquiry, committees, research and evaluation. Especially the last; while evaluation of students has remained under a cloud, in other areas an evaluative binge has settled into an industry. Evaluation of teaching; of administrators; of departments. My own department, as I recall offhand, has undergone within the past two years at least two full-scale external evaluations, plus an internal evaluation by a local committee; another external evaluation is to come this year, and now under way is an evaluation of the internal evaluating committee, all producing compendious reports.

It is inevitable perhaps that years of unrest should now stimulate a priority for peace at any price, the reconcilement of discord, the middle road, and the prize of stability. Moreover, in the mid-seventies, many university presidents are themselves young enough to have been impressed by the liberal romanticism of the sixties. Whatever the reasons, almost no university president during the disruptions (except Hayakawa of San Francisco State) was willing to proclaim that the job of his unit was academic education—learning, teaching and research, the fostering of thought and inquiry. And even now, when the risks of such a pronouncement are considerably less, I have still not heard it made.

The result of all this has been a paralysing doubt within the university about its purposes, and a new scepticism outside about its value and status, as many a new graduate, applying for his first job, has found. Such doubts extend to the highest levels. The Supreme Court, for instance, has declined to pronounce on the De Funis case, in which an applicant to a state law school found himself, despite a superior entrance record, rejected in favour of racial minority applicants of lesser academic achievement. Inside the university, the new god is hesitantly proclaimed: Innovation. It has replaced Relevance, but its hold is unsure, and its life will almost certainly be shorter than its predecessor's. But the most disturbing feature of all in the new Peace, and the product of the loss of intellectual discussion, is a broad range of intolerance. Often it is minor; a plan for an honours college for brighter students is vetoed by egalitarian radicals on governance committees; an innocuous motion by a 'conservative' dies for lack of seconding, only to be passed without dissent when proposed by an acceptable liberal; small, though symptomatic matters. There is, however, also a most serious anti-intellectual intolerance for which universities may expect to pay very dearly in the future. Debates and talks on the relation of genetics and intelligence have been cancelled because their implications have not been acceptable to the prevailing social orthodoxy, and this at Harvard as well as at several lesser institutions. The Berkeley administration is on record that research should be discouraged which 'may place the reputation or status of a social group or an institution in jeopardy'.[1]

This being so, free inquiry, without which the university cannot hope to recover its purpose, is itself in danger. And it is crucial to realize that the spiritless, disoriented atmosphere whose features I have sketched owes only a part of its existence to the barbarities of the sixties. The sixties, after all, were surface drama; the roots lie deeper, and it is time to question some simple basic assumptions which have been held sacrosanct for too long. They lie within the democratic concept of mass higher education on a huge scale; to put it crudely, in the idea that the methods of mass production form a valid analogy, where the product is

[1] Ronald Berman, *New York Times Magazine*, 10 February 1974, p. 19.

education. Since the American comprehensive high school set the pattern at the turn of the century, the pragmatics of 'mass education' have enforced, in increasing measure, a fatal inversion of emphasis—the sacrifice of the second word in the term to the first. The rest has followed inexorably: the elective system; the complex administration to deal with it; the lowered standards; substitutes for academics in life-adjustment and societal fashions. All are clichés of educational history in America, and recent realities in Britain. The consequence of this inversion of educational purpose—from stress on knowledge to stress on society—perpetually assumes what are merely new forms. In America at present, for instance, the idea of education as technological assembly-line product means that, while school libraries have usually been miserably funded for years, money is at the moment easily available for what is to replace them, the new 'learning resource centres' combining, according to one proponent, 'the efficiency of the modern supermarket with the service of the old-fashioned corner grocery'. Adroit librarians, by accepting some title like Director of the Multimedia Communications Centre, have been able, at least in the colleges, to lay hands on funds hitherto unavailable (and even to buy books with them if they are bold and discreet enough). The fatal inversion in Britain in the last decades, as in America earlier, has followed other predictable lines—broader, mixed-subject degree programmes for far more students; the growth of administration as a trade. Then, in both countries, when the sense of academic purpose had become sufficiently blunted, the late sixties proposed a substitute and apparently irresistible one, no less than the reform of society itself. The failure of that grail-quest is not important as such; it is notable in stressing yet again that there is only vacuum where a university's purpose ought to be.

The situation has been neatly summarized in a speech of April last year by President McGill of Columbia. He complained of 'the creation of large numbers of low-quality centres of higher education which entice students on the pretext that enrolment will enhance their employability. . . . We have thus created a ridiculous situation where a college degree is deemed necessary to be a policeman or to drive a truck or to operate a telephone switchboard.' Over-expansion, he remarked, has led to 'a rapid deterioration in the quality of four-year degrees at many public colleges and universities', and he added the warning that the universities 'must not become storage houses for bored young people'.[2]

'Storage houses for bored young people.' It is already, I believe, a fair description of what has been created by the American university's abandonment of its fundamental academic purpose. We are left with confused conglomerates which may in part fulfil one or another social or economic need, but which have no core to replace the erstwhile academic one. I return to my pathetically divided classes, one-third serious, two-thirds lost; they represent a long-term development, I would stress again, exacerbated, but not caused, by the troubles of the sixties.

It may be that we should frankly accept that what has been created cannot be realistically undone; that there is social, economic and perhaps psychological need for the conglomerates we have. We might accept them, continue to subsidize them, make them honest, and name them accurately: Political Awareness Camps, Labour Market Holding and Dispersal Units, Career Adjustment Clinics? The way might then be cleared for experiment, in a small way, with basics in school education—reading, writing, mathematics. It might be surprising in its effects (—perhaps even the ultimate, if indirect, improvement of society?) And perhaps there might be places where those committed to knowledge of the past, and its development in the future, to ideas, books, reflection, discussion, enlightenment, could indulge themselves in harmless directions. Until a better title occurs, they might even be called universities.

[2] *New York Times*, 30 April 1974, p. 50.

The Mining of the Ivory Tower

BERNICE MARTIN

In the 1960s the universities of western Europe and America were rocked by an upsurge of progressive radicalism, and then, in the 1970s, calm gradually crept back so that today, with the partial exception of West Germany, universities and students are no longer so newsworthy. The industrial disputes in mass higher education have cooled and production has been resumed. But it may be worth looking at the syndrome that characterized the disruption period and asking what deposit it has left in the apparently normalized university system which survived the inundation of radicalism.

My thesis is that 'the student revolution' was only one facet of a general cultural movement popularly known as the avant-garde or the counter-culture. It was one link in a chain of paradoxes the logic of which has not yet fully exhausted itself. Industrialization has produced, as Talcott Parsons has put it, first the Educational and then hard on its heels the Expressive Revolution. Western societies within the space of a mere century have moved through the stages of mass elementary and mass secondary education and are now entering the era of mass higher education. Industrialism and its resultant material affluence have created what Ralf Dahrendorf has called the Educational Class—that vast and growing army of teachers, lecturers, administrators and the like who staff the institutions of mass literacy and swell the ranks of the middle classes in industrial societies. More than this, it has become possible for modern societies to afford a large cultural class divorced from material productive processes and devoted to non-materialist and non-utilitarian pursuits of an artistic, intellectual and expressive kind. By expressive values and activities is meant all those things which are self-justifying by reference only to the intrinsic enrichment of experience which they afford (psychic, personal, emotional or intellectual) and not to what they produce or achieve (i.e. instrumental justification). Of course the more people are freed from daily uncertainty about basic material necessities the more possible it is for expressive values to surface in their consciousness. Ordinary folk can afford to become preoccupied with inherent satisfactions—the *quality* of marriage, friendship, parenthood, work, leisure, politics, etc.—and to be unsatisfied by mere survival. So expressive values as a yardstick by which to measure experience become more salient throughout society. But beyond this there has also evolved a whole stratum of society distanced and partially protected from the instrumental activities and material priorities of society's existence, and able by a characteristic process of institutional specialization to embody and assert the values of cultural and expressive primacy in human life. Psychiatry, much of the social and psychological welfare professions, the arts, the mass media and the entertainment industry all figure prominently in this stratum alongside education.

The counter-culture was in essence just a further differentiation within the cultural class itself: the *alter ego* of the established cultural élite. Both are equally parasitic on the world of materially productive work; in this sense both are the natural successors of the Church and universities of the pre-industrial era, though their numbers are vastly greater, their institutional focus much more diverse and their links with the structure of power more tenuous. At bottom the Expressive Revolution was an extravagant statement of the self-affirming and anti- or non-instrumental values of the new cultural class. The ideas and motifs of the counter-culture were not so much a radical break with conventional culture as the logical development of some of the central expressive values of that culture. The radical wing of the Expressive Revolution was making a bid for *absolute* autonomy for the new 'leisured class', for *total* divorce from the political and economic paymasters. The universities became the most spectacular battleground of the Revolution because they were strategically poised with a foot in both the expressive and the instrumental camps. The arts, even though they may sometimes assist in legitimating the *status quo*, are *inherently* expressive and therefore not intrinsically problematic for the forces of the Expressive Revolution. The 'hard' areas of economic and political expediency may be the logical target of the expressivist rebels, but they are well defended and significantly distant from the influence of the cultural class. The university (and to a lesser extent the school) is closer, less powerfully armed and the most obviously disputed territory. It is expected in part to service the labour market and the material, scientific and administrative needs of industrial society, and in part to bear witness to timeless human values—the pursuit of intellectual excellence and moral truth regardless of the consequences, of perfection, of spiritual and aesthetic insight, of innovation, of beauty, of personally satisfying uselessness.

At one level then, the Expressive Revolution is not in any necessary sense politically radical. Indeed its essence is to be *a*-political and *a*-economic, that is not to assert a *new* politics and economics but to affirm the supremacy of values other than those of politics and economics. In this sense the music students who went on playing their instruments and ignoring student assemblies throughout the troubles were more complete examples of the Expressive

Revolution than the philosophers and social scientists who ran the assemblies. At another level, of course, politics was a crucial part of the syndrome. Here one needs to introduce another consideration about the nature of radical politics in the sixties in Western Europe and North America. The degree of potential social conflict and political polarization in these societies is very varied: no modern western society is without its institutional focus of political protest and class antagonism. But two points need to be borne in mind. First the experience of Russian communism has made the Puritan and politically realistic variant of left-wing Utopianism very suspect (*a*) on nationalist and (*b*) on expressivist grounds: Eastern Europe is clearly no paradise of free-floating individualism as its own rebellious cultural class makes abundantly clear. Second the intellectual stratum rather than the proletariat always tends to articulate radical ideologies—this after all is part of the natural function of a leisured élite whose *raison d'être* is ideas. Ideological though not necessarily pragmatic political leadership therefore tends to be characteristically middle class. The more the cultural and educational class can be differentiated off from the hard areas of politics and economics the more likely it is that a substantial minority of this protected enclave will be contemptuous of and outraged by the political compromises, manœuvres and privileges of the ruling group: thus for many of them *every* politician, general and businessman *must* have his own Watergate to hide. So the phenomenon of middle-class expressive politics evolves: political action designed to express the value premises and manifest the moral cleanness of the participants rather than to achieve a concrete end.

For these among other reasons hard variants of radicalism—classical Marxist socialism, national socialism and doctrines of proletarian revolution—were relatively weak in the 1950s and '60s. The proletariat in even the most polarized western societies showed little or no sign of spontaneous combustion, and among the intelligentsia the Protestant ethic of work, diligence and control was discredited by its contamination with capitalism and bureaucracy, and was being replaced by a revamped Romantic individualism more in tune with expressive values. Political ideologies on the left accordingly tried the expedient of anarchic expressivism, preaching the conversion of souls through drugs, psycho-drama, sexual licence and the wholesale breaking of taboos in the hope of eroding the fabric of what Marcuse calls 'repressive tolerance'.

Now this syndrome contains a twin possibility—the politicization of culture or the transformation of politics into a system of purely symbolic gestures. The first makes the 'soft' areas of culture serve the 'hard' political battle, the second retreats from 'hard' politics and economics and takes refuge in the expressive arts, which then stand in for political action. In the first case anarchic techniques largely deriving from the arts—Dada, Surrealism and the ideology of Romantic individualism—are used aggressively as weapons of psychic subversion and political re-socialization by would-be revolutionary movements (usually of the left but it could just as easily as in the 1920s be the right). Continental Europe, particularly France and Germany, has had some recent experience of cultural politics of this variety, for the student revolutions of the mid- to late sixties took precisely this form. Alfred Willener's [1] account of the troubles at the Sorbonne in 1968 is a perfect example of the whole syndrome. The success of this tactic has been very limited even if one attributes to it the French Government changes after the 1968 student rebellions. Even in the most polarized Western European societies the main impact of the attempt to politicize culture has been confined to the universities and the radical intelligentsia.

[1] A. Willener, *The Action Image of Society*. Tavistock, 1970.

Much might be written about this Continental mode which has fused without much difficulty with several variants of Marxist ideas and tactics. However, I shall concentrate on the second mode which is more characteristic of Anglo-American cultural patterns. Here one finds not the politicization of culture but the politics of cultural symbolism. In this case radical politics merely translate themselves into a style of cultural gesture which employs the same anarchic techniques but primarily as a form of self-display and a badge of in-group solidarity among the progressive intelligentsia. When this happens anarchic expressionism becomes a cul-de-sac instead of the high road to revolution. The radicals avoid the 'hard', 'masculine', 'instrumental' areas of industrial and agricultural production, business, politics and administration. These are seen as citadels still too well rooted in the 'false consciousness' of all social classes to be easily toppled. Progressives in these societies therefore huddle together in the esoteric temples of élite culture (or counter-culture if you prefer). Through the arts they can preach to the converted, and symbolically reaffirm their mutual righteousness through cultural gestures the impact of which is largely confined to the avant-garde itself. Thus their chosen field of operation is the 'soft', 'feminine', 'expressive' areas of modern life, the arts, education, the 'caring' professions, etc., and part of my thesis is that in British and to a lesser extent American society, much of the revolutionary potential has been drained off into self-affirming orgies of expressivism among the radical middle classes. So Britain offers the world a Vanessa Redgrave instead of a Rosa Luxembourg, a John Lennon not a Lenin.

Yet there is still a further paradox. In spite of the self-induced political impotence of the avant-garde which results from their avoidance of the power centres of the economy and the polity, they have had a not negligible cultural impact. In most Western liberal societies progressives hold some of the commanding positions in educational institutions and the mass media, and hence can induct the norms and distribute the symbols of the Expressive Revolution to society at large.

At this point one must note some very crucial developments in the structure of the universities and indeed the whole system of higher education which began to play into this situation. As higher education is extended to an ever-expanding proportion of the population two important developments occur. First the universities are supplemented, and in some cases even swamped by other institutions whose *raison d'être* is less the embodiment of humanistic culture than the production of trained personnel for technological and other useful professional and semi-professional roles in society. The universities may either be infiltrated by the latter set of functions or may be specialized off as the 'purer' non-vocational and non-utilitarian institutions. There are dangers in both possibilities of course—in the first place the risk voiced so extravagantly by the Expressive Revolutionaries of the sixties that humanistic ideals may be distorted and corrupted by the pressures of immediate expediency, and in the second place the danger of being regarded as a socially irrelevant luxury and starved of funds and manpower by an instrumentally-oriented ruling establishment.

The second important feature of the universities of the mid-twentieth century is the fact that even when one has allowed for the impact of the other institutions of higher education, larger numbers of relatively underprivileged segments of the population begin to receive a university education with its systematic exposure to humanistic values which set themselves apart from and above mere utility. Now humanistic culture has traditionally meant élite

culture and its values are certainly most easily operable in the life-style of the wealthy, cultured gentleman: Renaissance man is essentially patrician. This has several interlocking consequences. It means that the universities retain an élite label while the new institutions of instrumental higher education are commonly granted less status deference in spite of their frequent efforts to become more like the traditional universities. The educationally mobile student of relatively lowly origins is more likely to find his way to the new vocational and technological institutions: the children of the privileged classes go in greater proportions to the humanist institutions. There is even an implicit status differentiation within subjects: the humanities and pure sciences—traditional gentlemanly subjects—carry more status than do applied science and technology or vocational subjects even within the universities themselves and are differentially popular with the students from privileged and professional strata. All this parallels the war within the middle classes between a pragmatic and a humanistic ethos.

Western education systems are so structured that the universities are intellectually the free-est and most humanistic sectors: they are ideally conceived of as devoted to the life of the mind for its own intrinsic and self-justifying sake. If knowledge *qua* knowledge can be pursued anywhere it is in the universities. It is true that traditionally universities have also concerned themselves with the vocational training of gentlemen or at least with the symbolic legitimation of fitness to enter the gentlemanly professions, and have never worried much about the vocationalism of medicine or law or divinity faculties as demeaning. But these were the old élite professions: the new technical professions of the industrial state are hived off where possible either to lower status technical institutions or to enclaves of postgraduate vocational training. Thus the universities have if anything *increased* their emphasis on education for its own sake and underlined their own definition of themselves as the main bastion of humanistic values in a materialist world dominated by economic and bureaucratic norms. Moreover they could in this century as well as the last usually count on the sympathy and support of the economic and political élite who, even if some were themselves philistines, had a traditional respect for gentlemanly culture and for the life of the mind as pursued by the best brains of their generation. Indeed they often saw this as in part at least the 'civilization' which morally justified the material success of modern industrialism.

Yet while the universities were specializing out the humanistic ethos they were also expanding with the mass education industry itself. Industrial societies more and more came to use (or believe they were using) education to sort out the various levels of talent and skill and assign the labour force to its 'appropriate' point of entry on the occupational hierarchy: more and more occupations required educational qualifications as an entry permit. So the universities found themselves at the apex of a system of occupational selection, with the vast majority of both the old and new upper status occupations expecting incumbents to have passed through a university degree before embarking on vocational training either on the job or in a specialized vocational course. Universities played along with this development to the extent that they justified and promoted their own vast expansion on the grounds (unsupported by anything other than rhetoric and extrapolation from existing trends) that modern societies 'needed' graduates.

Thus our middle classes pass through a very long process of formal education, the unequivocal ideal goal of which is academic pursuits for their own sake, culminating in three or more years of intensive socialization in humanistic values and life-style in the university. At this point society expects them finally to face the world of work—economics, bureaucracy, power, compromise, instrumentality, conflicting and only partly realized goals, time limits, compartmentalization and the rest. Is it any wonder that one of the favourite slogans of the L.S.E. student militants of the late sixties was: 'Who *wants* to join middle management at £1,500 a year?' The problem is that in our expanded universities life is a rather loose but tempting induction into a pattern of activities and values which cannot easily be exported intact into the outside world. It sows the seeds of a taste for the life of the ivory tower which can scarcely be satisfied except by staying there. But however many modern annexes it builds the ivory tower cannot accommodate all who would for preference take refuge there. The problem is worst in the humanities and social sciences, and least in science and technology where utility and vocation are more easily justified.

Here one needs to draw attention to two processes which affect these developments. The first is the process of self-recruitment in the cultural classes. Certain professions and occupations are more successful than others at distancing themselves from material and instrumental norms: these as we remarked earlier are *par excellence* the free-floating cultural professions in the arts, entertainment and the mass media, and to a modified degree the caring professions and the educational growth industry itself. Thus families already entrenched in these areas tend to predispose their children to follow the same circular route around the educational feeder plant back into the expressive professions. The second process which supplements this is the constant expansion of education and the expressive professions alike, so that each generation provides new recruits from lower status origins to join and extend the circular flow.

These two processes have important consequences. In the first place because of the circularity of the process the anti-instrumental ethos is self-confirming and likely to be exaggerated rather than modified over time. In the second place it gives rise to a phenomenon which one might call 'status drip'. As the system expands, so many of its products have to search lower down the status hierarchy for occupational niches. Exaggerated and crudified forms of humanistic values stripped of subtlety, complexity and fertilizing paradox are thus 'dripped' down to ever lower reaches of the occupational hierarchy so it becomes more accurate to refer to an 'anti-instrumental' rather than a positively 'humanistic' ethos at this point. One result of this, especially in the education system itself, is the persistent erosion and disconfirmation of the instrumental functions which the system partly exists to perform—occupational selection, the possibility of social mobility, the acquisition, assessment and measurement of skills, etc. A further result which the student troubles of the sixties materially assisted is the erosion of the confidence of the commercial and political classes that the universities or their lower-status analogues in the expressive half of the system are either safe or sensible investments: the paymasters begin to have nagging doubts as to whether there is either 'civilization' or 'use' to be found there.

We should now perhaps return to the counter-culture and the student troubles. Why did the explosions occur in the universities if they are, as the argument runs above, havens of protection for humanistic values and the gentlemanly life-style? The point is that, though the universities are the safest home for the children of the Expressive Revolution they are even so not pure havens of repose from the realities of twentieth-century industrial society: they still have their instrumental functions—in terms say of occupational selection, of status legitimation, recruitment to élite positions, practical pay-offs from research in natural and social science and so on. Moreover because they are part of a massive growth industry they cannot easily avoid taking on features which characterize modern bureaucracies—largeness of scale, impersonal administrative procedures, standardization, specialization, compartmentalization of operations and the like. Many of these features are bound to be encouraged by the political and economic paymasters in whose sphere they form part of the normal life-style: any other pattern will be under suspicion as inefficient and anachronistic. One should remember too that my description of the circular process of self-recruitment to the cultural classes involves an element of caricature: the circle is not perfect and some participants—often the new recruits—are imbued with models of modernity, progress and efficiency culled more from the economic than the humanistic enterprise. Or again the instrumental elements may be strategically emphasized as part of the rhetoric justifying the universities in terms that will convince the paymasters through a vocabulary they understand. Such strategies have a nasty habit of turning rhetoric into necessary fact as a *quid pro quo* for expansion, research funds or what you will.

Thus we see the universities as a fair field for battle between the humanistic/expressive and the pragmatic/ instrumental ethos. Although this was not the only factor in the situation, the Expressive rebels of the sixties could plausibly see themselves as so many Odysseuses slaughtering Penelope's suitors. They entered their only real home to find it polluted by alien intruders trying to take over the true master's functions. So we have thus far the first two of the series of paradoxes which describe the course of the mining of the ivory tower:

1 Industrialization creates and finances a leisured or cultured class which can then afford the luxury of despising and condemning the instrumentality and materialism of its creators.
2 The children of the Educational and Expressive revolutions use the counter-culture's extension of humanistic values to attack the only safe home of those values, the universities.

It may be worth examining the counter-culture in a little more detail as a logical extension of established values. What were its lines of continuity with and divergence from the traditional humanistic culture of the universities? Where the traditional values of humanism have always asserted the worth of the life of the mind and imagination outside the cash and power nexus, the counter-culture re-translated this into a total devaluation of any other kind of enterprise, in particular anything which was useful to a stratified and materialist industrial state. They replaced a distant respect for utility by a celebration of uselessness. Expressiveness became its own justification with a consequent preference for the ephemeral (and therefore immediate and personal) over the lasting (and therefore fixed and to that extent impersonal). Rationality and objectivity had been a crucial part of the universities' traditional understanding of humanism: these were the powers and disciplines by which the human mind could alone transcend animal immediacy and domination by instinctual and environmental forces. They were nevertheless rejected by the counter-culture as ideologically tainted through their association with bourgeois science, technology and bureaucracy: they were condemned as the bases of personal inhibition and psychic impoverishment and awarded only the creation of 'capitalism' to their doubtful 'credit'. So rationality and objectivity must go; in their place arose cults of anti-, non- or irrationality backed up by rhetoric derived from sources as diverse as Wordsworth, Nietzsche, de Sade, popularized post-Freudianism and the whole rag-bag of second-hand Romantic individualism. Instead of objectivity as an aim and positivism as a method, subjectivism and relativism came to prevail as the only adequate vehicle for expressing the uniqueness and diversity of humanity. So magic could become superior to science, and by one of many such ironies only reason came to be seen as truly sub-human.

Curiously certain forms of individualism were also casualties of the counter-cultural ideology despite the fact that 'doing one's own thing' regardless of convention was one of the treasured values of the anarchic radicals. Individualism in academic matters became suspect the moment it smacked of achievement orientation which again was polluted by its links with capitalistic competitiveness. So individualism was only acceptable as part of the cult of the loser, the deviant and the drop-out: individualists who were winners *ipso facto* 'must' have sold out to the System. And in this context loser-oriented 'individualism' was quickly indistinguishable from peer-group conformity. Tolerance of diversity, especially in politics, was similarly thrown out of the humanistic package. Liberal tolerance was seen as a patronizing confidence trick: it was the psychic violence of the powerful who had already socialized the powerless into rough conformity. Surface tolerance was the sneer of the Establishment at impotent minorities it didn't even need to martyr. And Herbert Marcuse coined the endlessly useful phrase 'repressive tolerance' to express the point and to justify the use of totalitarian repression and censorship by the enlightened against the conformist tools of the System.

Thus certain humanistic values were taken through the twists of their own logic to become their own opposites. Rationality turned to irrationality, objectivity to subjectivism and relativism, tolerance to 'justified' violence against the unenlightened, individualism became peer-group conformity, and intellectualism spawned anti-intellectualism to undermine the very foundations of the university's unique rationale. The life of the mind was well and truly blown.

The counter-culture had originally evolved not in the universities but in the so-called underground and in the avant-garde arts. In the sixties all these movements converged, and ideas which had been very esoteric for decades were by then ripe for popularization at the hands of the most foot-loose segments of the cultural class—protected adolescents and media operators in particular. Thus the counter-culture was assiduously proselytized by the student radicals (and some of their elders), by pop and the mass media. The motifs of the movement had been around for a very long time. At one level the source material was the politico-religious millenialism of proto-protestant anti-nomianism. This was supplemented and reworked by the Romantic movement and topped up by the anarchic and surrealist movements of the early twentieth century. And of course there were the obvious political inspirations of the left. The adepts of the counter-culture were sometimes Expressivist on principle—immediate experience as superior to the historic cumulations of culture or the hard-won skills of individual achievement—and sometimes on tactical grounds which favoured the use of techniques of psychic subversion designed to shock the conventional mind so that hitherto unquestioned regularities could be seen as 'absurd' instead of as intractable 'givens'.

The aspect of the counter-culture to which I want to draw particular attention is its essential hostility to structure. It attacked ritual, form, boundaries, categories, roles and certainties in every conceivable sphere. I have shown elsewhere the way in which this worked itself through in the avant-garde arts and pop music, both of which had crucial roles as vehicles of expression and simultaneous symbols of identity and protest for the student rebels. It may be worth summarizing briefly here the main recurrent themes.

The separate arts all produced their own modes of eroding or denying structure and became increasingly involved in multi-media enterprises which sought to break down the distinctions between the separate arts themselves and provide the social basis for the experience of group euphoria: what after all were Happenings if they were not instant ritual for the counter-cultural élite? Student demonstrations and protests had the same quality. The boundaries most frequently under attack were those between the public and the private sphere, between decent and indecent, tabooed and available, sacred and profane, between Art and ordinary life, good taste and vulgarity, between creator and creation, artist and observer, between human and inhuman, male and female, animate and inanimate, Man, Animal and Nature. The rejection of control in all its forms showed itself as a preference for randomness or chance over plan, for excess over balance, for the fantastic over the normal, for emotion over reason, for the ephemeral over the lasting, for immediacy over hard-won comprehension, for the purely personal or topical allusion over the historically rooted image.

So far as subject matter is concerned all the avant-garde arts were particularly intent on breaking the taboos concerning sex, violence and good taste. The body symbolism of sexuality is a particularly potent symbolic instrument: all orifices become infinitely penetrable, sex becomes public not private. This both attacks convention by breaking taboos and provides an easy focal point for avant-garde identity: the 'up-tight' are patently not enlightened. All the arts employed both the pastoral idyll and the daemonic in relation to sex—sex as 'natural' lyricism or sex as salvation through the ultimate degradation of the self and others. In literature for example this takes one from Lawrence through to Genet and Burroughs. There was widespread use of sexual ambiguity, and of what would be conventionally regarded as sexual perversions: another barrier to fall was that between art and pornography. Much of this involved the sanctification of violence, even paradoxically, when one was preaching an end to violence. The other most favoured taboo which the avant-garde delighted in violating was that which protects high culture from vulgarity—from culturally 'low' forms like advertising, *grand guignol*, the horror film or pop music. Thus 'camp' became a cherished part of avant-garde culture providing the opportunity for the superior sneer, sado/masochistic immolation in vulgarity, and the key to the identity of fellow members of the progressive élite all at the same time. The cult of the object also assisted in eroding the distinction between art and the everyday or commonplace: the new novel with its minute and seemingly irrelevant details of material objects, the 'objet trouvé' as sculpture, Duchamp's 'readymades' and so on.

As well as themes which are common to all the arts there are concerted attacks upon accepted style and form in each separate sphere, so that what one might call the grammar and punctuation of the various arts was largely discarded in favour of free, structureless expression.

The avant-garde arts and pop music flowed naturally into student radicalism providing the latter with themes and perspectives and above all a vocabulary. Both in terms of fashions in taste and in terms of models of behaviour, the motifs summarized above were at the heart of the counter-culture's onslaught on the universities. Many of the ideas could be translated straight into educational panaceas for purifying the social system of the universities and the intellectual content and packaging of the education on offer. Thus for example the student rebels sought to eliminate the distinction between teacher and taught in all kinds of ways—by demanding an equal say in curriculum content, by either eliminating or participating in assessment methods, by taking control of student recruitment and staff appointments, by abolishing or invading separate staff dining and common rooms, studies and offices, by denying the staff the right to privileged access to personal information about students and colleagues. Many of these demands also constituted a denial of the distinction between public and private (places, information, behaviour, roles) between relevant and irrelevant (knowledge, roles) between different subject areas (no departments, faculties, or expertise) between cognition and feeling, between 'book knowledge' and random sense impressions, between high culture and triviality or vulgarity, between the university and the outside world—thus occupying a public park or squatting in empty property 'for the people' could be regarded as at least as valid as academic work in defining the students' proper role. 'Are you a sociologist or a human being?' was the persistent opening gambit of one of my own students during this period. The boundaries between individuals were symbolically attacked in innumerable ways—conventional, role-distinctive forms of address were dropped, instant personal intimacy was claimed, the protective walls around private or vulnerable parts of the personality were indignantly assaulted. The concept of academic production as individual private property in knowledge was anathema to many radicals and gave way to the collective project: thus as late as 1974 Dr Halsey could receive a collective essay from fifteen self-styled Maoist students in one British university.[2]

Curiously enough while the assault on boundaries was producing undifferentiated group phenomena like this, certain selected boundaries and categories were given a new salience. In particular the conventional academic assumption that all scholars are in a certain sense equal and alike through their acceptance of basic humanist and intellectual norms met resistance on the new grounds of subjectivism, relativism and the superior worth of the underdog. Thus women and ethnic minorities in particular came to be treated as special ascriptive categories with their own world view, value system and self-oriented subject matter. Women's studies, black studies and the like deny the possibility of objectivity, comparability and equality in scholarship.

In many of the examples noted above one sees individualist and anarchic notions twisting on their axis to become collectivism of various kinds. In part this is a consequence of the assault on boundaries and structure: without boundaries distinctiveness is unattainable. But it was a result too of a basic dilemma which the whole counter-culture built into its own position. They were caught in a permanent and unresolvable tension within their own ideology between motifs of structurelessness and the need for symbols and rituals expressing their own collective identity. They employed the language of what Mary Douglas has called 'zero structure'.[3] But zero structure as a rhetorical ploy is very different from zero structure as a life pattern. It is one thing to attack the rituals, roles, boundaries, limits and structures of other men's systems when you see them as the prison bars of convention and inauthenticity, but it is quite a different matter to pursue pure zero as one's own life pattern, consisting as it must of fleeting or tangential human contacts and weak or non-existent bonds.

Most student radicals—and indeed most initiates of the wider counter-culture—really hoped to replace old, conventional structures ('artificial' and/or 'evil') by a new community ('real', 'natural' and 'good'). Here one encounters a bifurcation in the counter-culture which echoes that between gentle Utopian and violent adventist millenialism, or between the pastoral and the daemonic wings of Romanticism. In the former case it is held that the dissolution of existing restrictive structures in academic, social and personal life will clear the way for the natural earth-harmony to assert itself which only perverse human meddling is preventing. In the latter case the belief is that most of mankind is (for the moment at least) doomed to inauthenticity, while alone the enlightened individual or chosen élite has the power to ride the daemonic forces of the human psyche, social development, history, nature or whatever. The road to illumination and salvation for the saints is often the path of excess, and if they see themselves as the Lord's sword to scourge the unrighteous then this variety of radicalism seldom sees beyond Armageddon to the New Jerusalem. In Britain and America, most student radicals were in the last analysis almost exclusively the former type, gentle retreatists. Continental Europe suffered more serious adventist millenialism of the latter type.

The rhetoric and praxis of zero structure brought dilemmas and contradictions for both styles of radicalism. The main problem is that if one's whole symbolic system is geared to attacking ritual and structure *as such*, it becomes immensely difficult to prevent the natural logic of such a stance from undermining all one's attempts to breathe life into the community principle. If the dogma of zero structure is taken too seriously it can result in frustration rather than liberation. Instead of the prison of convention one may find the lonelier prison of self unconnected with other thrashing and alien selves, all incapable of building the arches of human communication because the acid ideology of liberation has destroyed the building materials. The unhappy experiences of some new universities founded on all the best progressive ideas may be explicable in these terms.[4]

One can of course achieve a pseudo-resolution of the dilemma by stylizing and restricting the motifs of structurelessness to a narrow range of symbols, so that they act as a badge of belonging: another middle-class student fashion like Afro hairdos, John Lennon specs, patched jeans or Viet-cong headbands. These intellectual, verbal, visual and political fashions then become mere peer-group convention, the essential prerequisite of staying in the social race, labels worn to show one has rejected all labels. A good deal of the student protest of the sixties was of this type of course: what else can one expect but conformity and tribalism of this sort if society isolates adolescent peer-groups in ever larger numbers on our still-expanding campuses?

The radicals wanted personalized experience not impersonal submergence in the mass, they valued expressive not instrumental values, they sought openness and spontaneity rather than closed, formal and inhibited contacts between human beings: they wanted to belong to a community not to be cogs in an institutional machine. But they treated expressive values rather as if they were water, a life-giving force. They saw society as if it were a landscape cut through by rivers and canals, dykes and dams. If water is good then restrictive channels must be bad, their argument ran. Too often they failed to see that without the canals and dykes the landscape would be less fertile: if they were removed the lack of barriers merely caused destructive floods drowning landscape and man alike.

[2] A. H. Halsey, 'Personal Column'. *Times Higher Education Supplement*, 9 August 1974.
[3] M. Douglas, *Nature Symbols*, Barrie and Rockliffe, 1970. See also M. Douglas, *Purity and Danger*, Barrie and Rockliffe, 1966.
[4] See, for example, Mary Douglas's own analysis of what went wrong at the University of Essex in a letter to *The Times*, 3 August 1974.

In fact one can seldom find cases of social systems which provide their members with a deep-rooted sense of belonging except through the medium of clear and all-embracing role specification. If you want to belong you must know your place. Yet the student radicals wanted belonging without role specificity and constriction. The history of medieval sectarianism and of contemporary commune experiments points the same lessons. If the principle of group belonging triumphs then the end product is usually a totalitarian system more like the total institutions of prison, army or monastery than the looser conventional structures of ordinary society. If the internal contradiction is maintained then rituals of group belonging will evolve, expressing collective euphoria and emphasizing badges of belonging and internal equality at the expense of real individuality. This was one of the most potent sources of all the fashionable cults of Indian mysticism, with and without drugs, in which individualized ecstasy was the sense of fusion of the One with the All. But social systems resting on such foundations tend to be ephemeral: task orientation which at the very minimum is necessary to cope with the exigencies of continuity, is well-nigh impossible to achieve in so unstructured a milieu. When social disintegration ensues, as it often does, a counter-movement may spring up emphasizing clear role structures, simple but demanding criteria of belonging, certainty in place of drift. Thus the Jesus movement could sweep like wildfire through the campuses in the wake of hippy anarchism.

Though neighbourhood community normally rests on clear and indeed rigid role structuring, there is another model available and at least sometimes appropriate to a university: the model of the family can embody a more flexible and less rigidly ascriptive pattern of behaviour. The family after all is the main sphere of expressive behaviour in the modern world. While it rests on age- and sex-based role specifications, the family nevertheless allows for flexible development and highly personal and idiosyncratic remoulding of the basic social masks. The most successful traditional universities operate socially in something of the same way. Common socialization, shared values, smallness of scale, careful initiation into a personalization of role playing, and a subtle combination of role and status differentiation alongside selected symbols of common scholarly endeavour can combine in a delicate balance of ritual distancing and personal spontaneity. These are the safest homes of humanistic values. The model is very difficult to reproduce in a large-scale university however: the multi-versity or the mass university cannot easily resemble a small and beautiful Oxford college. The large university is therefore trapped between massification and bureaucratization on the one hand, and well-intentioned experiments in structurelessness on the other which are almost inevitably doomed to create maximum discontent and distress. There is no easy solution but it is quite clear that any serious erosion of roles, categories, limits and rules is a recipe for disaster, though what the exact *content* of these roles, categories, limits and rules should be is another and a far from self-evident matter.

These considerations also help to explain the chronological sequence of student troubles. Let us take some cross-cutting hypotheses:

1 Other things being equal high-status and therefore heavily humanistic/expressive universities are likely to produce counter-cultural minorities most easily.
2 Smallness of scale and personalization of operations will largely counteract the effects of 1.
3 Large-scale and traditionless new universities emphasizing humanistic/expressive values are very likely to produce sizeable counter-cultural minorities.

4 In the case of 3 the difficulties will be maximized by (a) bureaucratization and depersonalization or (b) progressive policies which erode role specificity and internal structuring.
5 In the case of 4(b) or other cases of institutional pursuit of structurelessness, the situation will be aggravated by the tendency to self-recruitment: the more an institution appears to favour the values approved by the counter-culture the more members it will attract who hold or flirt with progressive ideology.

Thus in America it was not Yale and Harvard but Berkeley which predictably proved front runner and in Britain it was not Oxbridge but London and the new 'progressive' universities. The spread of the pattern can largely be explained as an example of 'status drip', so that today in Britain the fashion has percolated down to a few remaining polytechnics with a high social-science component and to the schools and in America to the smaller state colleges and high schools.

And so finally what were the consequences for the universities of the counter-cultural revolution? Though the troubles have to some extent receded, they have altered many universities both in their social organization and in their curricula and course-structuring. As I insisted at the beginning of this paper, the student counter-culture was only an exaggerated manifestation of a more general phenomenon—the Expressive Revolution. For this among other reasons its motifs had a wider resonance in the culture at large than the sheer numbers of serious revolutionaries could possibly account for. Many of its ideas, popularized, vulgarized and adulterated, have passed into the common currency, and at another level still affect the intellectual fashions and academic predilections in the universities. Positivism, objectivity and reason are still widely suspect. Theories and philosophies stressing subjectivity and relativism are now entirely respectable. In sociology, to give only one example, phenomenology and ethnomethodology may have had a long history in German philosophic thought, but it took the university troubles of the 1960s to raise them alongside the accepted classics as a normal part of the curriculum.

The final paradox of the series is in many ways the saddest as well as the most inevitable. The major consequence of the radical sixties has been to strengthen the thrust of the bureaucratic ethos at the expense of the traditionalist and personal. If one looks at the fate of all those wild demonstrations to inaugurate student choice, flexible, personally tailored curricula and assessment methods (or none at all), student participation in decisions and the rest, one finds that every one of them has altered the university system in a mechanistic and bureaucratic direction. More committees, minutes, documents and bureaucratic prose. Fewer integrated subjects and more mechanized 'choice'—modular degrees, course units and the like. A multiplicity of types of assessment which range from the dissertation and the course essay (encouraging either the commercialization of cheating or the total relativization of assessment) through to 'objective testing' and other forms of programmed and mechanized assessment, all increasing the burden on student and staff alike.

The Expressive Revolution achieved its most extravagant institutional flourish in a decade in which it still looked as if material progress was automatic, and standards of living would go on rising effortlessly and indefinitely. At the popular level Western societies had not then seriously faced the possibility of zero material growth and retrenchment in living standards. Indeed many of the radicals believed that we were on the verge of an era in which all work could be relegated to machines and computers freeing human beings for 'life'. Pure expressiveness as a way of life looks less plausible on a large scale in the mid-seventies than it did in the sixties. Moreover expressiveness in all sorts of fields had been pushed to its own self-destructive limits and had nowhere new to go. Even more crucially it had lost its exclusiveness: by the late sixties it was no longer the preserve of the upper reaches of the cultural class but had passed down into popular culture.

Despite popularization and diffusion, however, the stronghold of the Expressive Revolution remains the cultural class in the education system and the freer-floating professions. Its destructive potential is far from spent, especially as the 'status drip' phenomenon percolates through to the lower reaches of the expressive occupational structure. It may be worth looking briefly at some of the effects of this in the schools before concluding this analysis.[5]

For some decades now progressive reforms have been eroding boundaries, categories, roles, rules and rituals in primary and secondary education. The social structure and the intellectual enterprise of the schools are both affected by these developments. In part destructuring movements have been an assertion of the superiority of openness and expressiveness over structure and instrumentality: in part they have been a reaction against anything, however contingent, which has happened to be historically linked with élite education. Thus for example, all-in schools are replacing selective ones, and co-education is squeezing out the single-sex school. Architectural boundaries are swept away in open-plan schools, subject boundaries are eroded in new subject groupings. Ideologically the stress has moved away from the pupil as recipient or apprentice to an insistence on his self-determination. Learning through exploration, feeling, and self-discovery replaces a notion of education acquired via a hierarchy of skills, structured by rules, sequence and ritual, and presided over by the teacher or expert whose authority to lead rests on his superior knowledge and training. At the same time all those things which traditionally embodied and expressed collective identity, group symbols such as uniform, Speech Day, school sports and the like, are out of favour. Hierarchy, authority, and honourable, achieved leadership roles are equally frowned on; instead peer-group authority gets ever new forms of expression both formal and informal in the school system.

Clearly these trends are more fully developed in some parts of the education system than in others, and the results in practice are very varied. It may however be worth point-

[5] For a fuller analysis see B. Martin, 'Progressive Education versus the Working Classes'. *Critical Quarterly*, Winter 1971.

ing to some of the more problematic consequences of the Expressive Revolution in our schools. In the first place one finds the same danger of anti-intellectualism that we noted in the counter-culture of the universities if the devaluation of the cerebral as against the emotional/expressive goes too far. There is too a serious danger of imprisoning children inside the philistinisms of local peer-group culture: in schools as well as universities the favoured mode of self-determining individualism all too often turns into peer-group conformity and in these cases only strong adult authority can protect and hedge about the precarious autonomy of the nonconforming child. The danger is probably worse for the child from a non-academic household whose only source of alternative cultural potential is school. The tendency to devalue useful skills because they are vocational and instrumental will also be more detrimental to working-class than to middle-class children because they above all *need* specific competences and not just sensitive souls with which to confront the labour market. Moreover the free-floating, unstructured social vocabulary of the progressive/expressive school is quite likely to be experienced as alien and disorienting by the typical working-class child whose family operates within a ritualized and highly structured life-style. In such a context the working-class child may well find it harder to acquire definable skills than he would in a more structured system: after all one can only successfully expand and supplement a person's *existing* emotional and cultural vocabulary; traumatic replacement seldom works without appalling cost. Of course many middle-class children outside the expressive professions may find a radically unstructured milieu difficult to cope with too, but at least they can pick up basic educational skills and motivation from home. Thus one of the more paradoxical net effects of the Expressive Revolution in the schools is to load the dice more than ever against the child from a working-class family—a sad harvest for an anti-élitist movement.

Whatever may be the case in schools—and there is some slight indication of disenchantment with the extremer forms of the progressive mode—the universities must continue to live with the consequences of the Expressive Revolution of the 1960s. Its institutional residue in their systems of government, their intellectual preoccupations and their informal social arrangements are far from negligible, but the greatest danger to the universities of the 1970s is the steady infiltration of the bureaucratic mode, of short-term utility, and pragmatic exigency, as the price they progressively pay both for their own expansion and as an ironic retribution for their pursuit of conspicuous uselessness in the 1960s.

ILEA Confidential

Edited by KINGSLEY AMIS and ROBERT CONQUEST

The following is a transcript of a tape-recording which appears to have been made inadvertently, and which has come into our hands in a way which cannot at present be disclosed. While we are as yet unable to vouch unreservedly for its authenticity, it does cast a more plausible light on recent educational decisions in London than most current explanations.

We have arbitrarily labelled the voices (apart from that of the obvious Chairman-figure) with letters of the alphabet.

CHAIRMAN Today, no doubt owing to the flu epidemic, we have the pleasant situation that, though there is a quorum, none of the human members or staff of the I.L.E.A. are with us. We can therefore relax—to the extent even, I suggest, of resuming our natural forms.
[*A slithering noise*]

CHAIRMAN [*an approximation only. All such transcriptions herein are approximate.*] Xtll p'bmorrra zan zannu . . .

VOICE A As most of us have spent decades on this planet, and are perhaps a little rusty in the Imperial High Speech, I move that we proceed in English.

VOICE B I second that. And, moreover, *Eye-elleeyay*, a collocation of syllables we can hardly avoid, is a subversive obscenity in the High Speech.

VOICE C It is in English too!
[*A series of rapid clicks and rumbles—?laughter*]

CHAIRMAN I agree. I put it to the vote . . . Thank you— carried by a show of pseudopods.—Nevertheless, let us begin proceedings with a formal obeisance to the Holy Emperor. Our Mother Star, Betelgeuse, is now on the eastern horizon. If all will turn in that direction . . . Anzz anzz upollolla na rrumu . . .

ALL Na rrumu.
[*We here omit 2 mins 53 secs of similar exchanges*]

CHAIRMAN In the circumstances, we will not bother with the Agenda: I will compose suitable Minutes later. This is, however, a useful opportunity for me to address you in my Imperial capacity, as Political Officer.

I think some of us tend to regard our task on this planet as tedious and unimportant compared with what is being done elsewhere to extend the Empire. But we must remember—

VOICE D Tedious is right! When are we going to see some action? I'm sick of all these Resolutions and Directives!
[*Some buzzing sounds, perhaps indicating agreement*]

VOICE A If I may . . . My dear Tormentor-General, we all know of your magnificent performance on Rigel II— what was it, 18 billion intelligent beings incinerated?— but you must bear in mind that our objective on Earth is quite different.

VOICE B I think too that the General underestimates our difficulties here, what with the loss of most of our Expeditionary Force in transit.

CHAIRMAN It was that factor, you recall, General, that led us to try to extend our activities through the use of synthetic creatures or androids. It is most lamentable that the experimental model was so lacking in verisimilitude, particularly as regards the facial movements, and could not be rationally controlled. Nevertheless, now it's been turned loose, it does seem to be helping to cause confusion in a small way in other circles, under the name Toniben.

VOICE C Great Pdahrg! On television recently it insisted it was human twice in the same minute. At that rate of over-compensation I don't see it lasting long.

CHAIRMAN No doubt. As I was saying, our task may seem slow, but, when it is finished, Earth will have become a luscious farm and mankind a self-renewing herd of high-protein meat-animals sufficient to feed half the Empire. We know that essential work to this end is being done by our fellow-servants of the Holy Emperor in the political leaderships on other parts of the planet. Yet the destruction of Western civilization, so called, is the key to final success. And our own share of that undertaking here in London ranks high.

I will not rehearse all our achievements. Still, who would have believed, even a few years ago, that we could have got away with such triumphs as diverting money and teachers into special centres where truants can devote themselves to—I quote our Spokesman— 'impromptu music, dancing, dressing up, cinema, lighting fires, painting and playing games'!
[*Clicks and rumbles*]

CHAIRMAN That is one of *this* year's accomplishments. For two or three years now we have been getting the public accustomed to, for example, schoolchildren's strikes and demonstrations. And here I want to emphasize an important point . . .

VOICE E [*slow and clumsy in tone*] What were they . . . demonstrating about?

CHAIRMAN Well, things like victimization.

VOICE E What's that?

VOICES Punishment!

VOICE E Well, if they can get away with it, you can't blame them. I . . . suffered just the first of the Eighteen Punishments once, and my pseudopods have never—

VOICE C Look, we know all about your brain injury on landing, but surely—

CHAIRMAN Order, please. In this case, punishment means being kept in for half an hour or something of that sort.

However, to continue. Our chief education officer issued a statement on the strikes and other encouraging activities, saying that it was important to give 'due consideration to legitimate views of pupils, some of whom may have been involved in recent events': and this was in rebuking two headmasters who proposed taking action against their charges!

The point here is that we aren't simply in the business of destroying London's educational system. Of course we are proud of the fact that reading ages in our area are already ten months behind the national average. Naturally we are delighted with the bad blood and general trouble caused by transferring children to and fro between schools, particularly when this is contrary to their parents' wishes. Naturally, too . . . Have you a point?

VOICE B I was merely anxious not to leave uncommemorated the current plan to create a comprehensive from two schools separated by the most dangerous crossroads in London.

CHAIRMAN Well taken—an outstanding case of getting everything right. I was going on to express our pleasure at truancy and indiscipline. What a heartening report that was the other day about a formerly 'good' school where the number of chairs smashed per annum is two and a half per child!

VOICE A Agreed, Mr Chairman, but we have no cause for complacency. Can we in London match the record of the 11 year old Bradford schoolboy who committed 51 burglaries and other thefts in a month? And the Empire has only a single Psychotechnical Sergeant there!

VOICE D Splendid fellow! Deserves a decoration!

CHAIRMAN Er, yes. Let me turn now to teachers. Alongside the presence of desirables who claim that violence in schools is caused by the presence of authority and of pressure to learn, we have the highly satisfactory and steadily growing shortage of teachers willing to work in our system.

VOICE A What about getting rid of 'good' ones who persist in actually trying to teach and keep order?

CHAIRMAN There are ways, and we have our allies. Look at the abrupt dismissal from his headmastership of the miscreant Rhodes Boyson upon his election to Parliament. There's no such hurry to be rid of progressives, you may be sure.

VOICE E Sorry, er . . . progressives?

VOICE C For Pdahrg's sake!

CHAIRMAN Order, order. A progressive teacher is one of ours, of course. Now: above all, I draw your attention to the remarks made in our name, which I was quoting a few minutes ago. We are not only producing illiteracy and animal conduct among children. We are getting the population as a whole quite accustomed to hearing meaningless bleats instead of their rational language. Another excellent example came at the time when we suppressed the yearly carol-singing festival. The explanation, you may remember, was that the children should 'have a more liberated style of folk-song'. Again, 'self-expression', that sturdy old standby, continues to serve us well.

VOICE A Won't someone notice some time that a lot of people—their Kipling, for instance—were exposing that one 60 years ago?

VOICE C They would have to be able to read to find that out!

[*Clicks and rumbles*]

CHAIRMAN At any rate, we now have it accepted that an allegedly adult body, as well as acting anti-socially, can *talk* in this way too. I think we can all be particularly proud of a remark made in *The Evening News* of Tuesday, 11 June 1974 by its columnist Miss Angela Ince. She noted a number of what I think we may call our cleverest ploys, and concluded with the following remarkable words: 'I.L.E.A.'s grasp of logic is comparable to that of a labrador puppy.' And that, my fellow-servants of the Holy Emperor, is precisely the level to which we are working to bring—and over the decades laid down in the Imperial Plan will succeed in bringing—the entire human race. I should add that she specifies a '*six-month-old* labrador puppy'.

[*Clicks and rumbles*]

CHAIRMAN I propose, with your approval, to include this testimony to our endeavours in a Special Despatch to the Emperor's Secretariat.

[*Buzzing sounds*]

VOICE B Mr Chairman, urgent: my psychoprobe indicates the approach of a human, speed 2.9 k.p.h., distance 37 metres and closing.

CHAIRMAN All present, please resume your human forms.

[*A slithering noise*]

CHAIRMAN A useful discussion, I think, ladies and gentlemen. A fruitful exchange of views. I look forward to the fulfilment of—

[*Sound of door opening and closing*]

CHAIRMAN Ah, good morning [*name unintelligible*]. I trust your influenza has relaxed its grip?

VOICE F Er? Yer, I'm a bit better now, thanks, Bert, I mean Fred. You boys been up to anything?

CHAIRMAN Ha ha, nothing out of the way.

VOICE F Er. Well, I got something out of the way, in a manner of speaking. I was on the phone to the Ministry just now, and according to what I heard, the grammar schools are going to be—

[*The tape breaks off at this point*]

Signs
of the Times

1 Strain on Teachers in Comprehensives

It is high time somebody made a tally of the casualties in our comprehensive schools—the shell-shocked, the battle-weary, the walking wounded—I refer, of course, not to the children but to the teaching staff . . . When did the Sheer Size of the Thing first raise its ugly head? When they took us from three compact, manageable, happy schools (small grammar, two secondary moderns) of under 450 pupils each, and herded us into this unwieldy affair of 1,500 pupils, now fast approaching 2,000.

Simply getting from A to B, which in the previous schools was no more than a pleasant stroll, is now something of an endurance test. To get from the main entrance to such far-flung outposts as the music centre or design department, can take fifteen minutes. . . .

In the smaller schools most of us tended to feel guilty if we were off for a day or two, knowing that somebody else would have to carry the load. Here it is possible to be off at the drop of a hat, and nobody seems either to know or care . . .

New members of staff receive no more than a cursory glance, and sometimes two or three terms have gone by before you even spot them. . . . The effect of this on the teaching staff is, first, psychological. If you lose your sense of individuality because of the sheer size of the staff-room, you become even more of a nonentity as far as the children are concerned . . . In the comprehensive set-up it takes us far longer to get to know the children, and most of the children never get to know more than a few of the staff.

But the physical effect is what bothers most of us. The nervous and bodily exhaustion, the enervation at the end of each week, the dog-tiredness at the end of each term, the relentless accumulation of stress . . .

The Times Educational Supplement, January 1974

2 Standards and Discipline in London

Examination results of London schoolchildren this year will be sub-standard. Some sixth formers who would have qualified for university entrance under last year's school conditions, this year will not. Even more boys who would have qualified for apprenticeships in the past, this year will not.

However rough and ready examination results may be as an indicator of the success or otherwise of an education service, they are one measure. They will reinforce the claim that London schools are now in a crisis situation . . .

Typical again was a group of young teachers who virtu-ally all said they were disillusioned with teaching in London secondary schools, and could not do the job they were trained for because of the lack of discipline in the schools. Nine out of ten said they would leave the London service at the end of their probationary year. The worst admission was that none was prepared to put in a personal complaint about their school—because it would blight their promotion prospects.

How on earth did the London schools, that were once the goal of young teachers, reach this state?

John Fairhall, *The Guardian*, January 1974

3 Uses of Obscenity

There are a number of comprehensive schools in London—some of them in more or less middle-class areas—where obscene language and graffiti are ubiquitous. These are not simply the occasional manifestations in the play-grounds and lavatories, or as part of a natural taboo-testing stage of adolescence; they are scrawled on chairs, desks and walls. Obscenities appear in English written work and classroom discussion. Sometimes, it seems, the children do it to shock; often they no longer know they are doing it since it is their mode of speech. Four-letter words are used freely by girls as well as boys which is no doubt encouraged by the fact that they are sometimes to be found in the books which they are given to read in English classes. If some teachers try to check this sort of thing, they are undermined by others, a minority of whom see nothing to worry about, and more of whom find it easier to swim with the tide.

This sort of thing can be manifest even in schools where the academic standards seem to be quite good and where the attitude of the headteacher is both dutiful and con-cerned. In one such school, where a good many of the children come from the more 'progressive' variety of middle-class homes, the headmaster has only been known to speak once about the prevalence of obscene language. For this there seem to be two reasons.

First, some of the teachers use the same language in their common rooms, just as a few of the teachers affect to dress like tramps. And in this trend the abolition of school uni-form is not insignificant. Children can now come to school dressed anyhow (a few from middle-class homes deliberately come barefoot) and with provocative 'badges' (often carrying obscene slogans) attached to their clothes, and it is not easy for teachers who would like to preserve some standards to draw the line—especially when some of their own number are as messy as the children. So it is difficult to say too much honestly and without imposing double standards. Second, so far as obscene and abusive language is concerned, it is frequently so excessive that anyone who seeks to check it may find it such an endless task that he gives up.

Ronald Butt, *The Times*, June 1974

4 Comprehensive Disaster

First: Comprehensive and bright children. Dr Bruce Chopin, research officer for the Government-backed National Foundation for Education Research, says after a major study of comprehensives:

'In five years' time there will be no chance of an Oxford or Cambridge scholarship for children who do not go to either our public, direct grant or top grammar schools.'

His findings showed that the standards of the brightest children at comprehensives are being hit hard and they are rapidly dropping out of the race for places at our top universities.

Already dons at Oxford have had to start a special system for talented comprehensive schoolchildren to by-pass the traditional entry route—because they fear they would not stand up to the competition from public and other top schools.

Secret estimates by the Ministry of Education also show a fall in the numbers of sixth formers expected to be good enough to go to university or college.

And these are confirmed by findings in Manchester, where the Labour-controlled council has discovered that 'O' level passes have slumped by 20% in the last four years.

Results over the same period from the non-comprehensive church schools have continued to increase rapidly.

Few parents will tolerate for much longer the vague promise that their bright children's education will not be harmed by shipping them into poor quality comprehensives.

Second: Comprehensives and behaviour. The evidence is now that comprehensives are failing on this count, even more disastrously than on academic standards.

A recent Government report called *Looking Forward to Employment* showed that 16 year olds leaving comprehensives were more bored, discontented, less happy and more likely to play truant than their counterparts in the old secondary moderns.

These are the children who were supposed to benefit most from the comprehensive revolution—yet a staggering 25% of them regularly play truant.

Third: Comprehensives and size. The theory was that the bigger they were the more they would be able to do for children—but the practice is proving very different.

Max Wilkinson, *Daily Mail*, September 1974

5 A Questionnaire for Teachers

What comes out clearly from the replies of the young teachers is a cry for help. Some seem to be almost in a state of shock. There are repeated references to 'stress' and 'strain' and several comments on the lines of 'the public just does not realize how hard a job London teachers have'.

'Two of my closest friends here in the hostel left London at Christmas due to discipline problems,' writes one 25–30 year old head of a secondary school department. 'Both first year teachers. One is still in hospital after a complete nervous breakdown.'

A medical welfare officer for Inner London teachers is suggested, and 'a psychological help service for teachers struggling under the mental and nervous stress of teaching in London'. More support from the older experienced teachers is asked for—a 'father figure' as one puts it, but not the headmaster, to whom a young teacher can turn for practical advice.

One of those leaving London writes: 'I am fed up with the abuse and the lowering of standards in London schools. How are we expected to teach when there is low motivation, low standards of English both among the English and immigrant children? I am not a racialist but please inform me how to teach a child the basic rudiments of science when he cannot understand English.'

John Fairhall, *The Guardian*, March 1974

6 'The Times' Speaks for Parents

It is no longer easy to believe that comprehensive education in itself markedly increases equality of opportunity among schoolchildren, even where, as the principle demands, neighbouring selective schools have been prevented from carrying away the cleverest. Parents are preoccupied with quite different concerns, to which the controversy over selection is of limited relevance. If it is too simple to allege that there is a direct causal link between the spread of the comprehensive school in London and the simultaneous spread of indiscipline, truancy and vandalism, there is at least as much truth in that association as there is in Mr Ashley Bramall's claim on Tuesday that the end of selection would bring a beneficial 'total transformation' to the comprehensives.

It is probably true that the pupils that London's state schools have to cope with are on average less able than those outside the capital, as well as more disgruntled, unruly and defiant. Partly this is because the area's private schools and numerous surviving grammar schools do take many of the most able. But unless the comprehensives that replace them can offer a reasonably comparable standard of schooling, then the abolition of grammar schools is more likely to feed the private sector and accelerate the flight of the middle classes from inner London than to fill the big schools with brighter, keener pupils as Mr Bramall implies.

The truth is that London comprehensives are very widely mistrusted, for reasons both good and bad. They are so large that they tend to acquire a demoralizing impersonality, unless their staff are of an unusually high calibre. The stresses of working with deprived children are such that the teachers are, on the contrary, very often novices far out of their depth. In a large and unselective school a minority of wild pupils can cause much wider disruption than they would have done in an old secondary modern. Many parents feel that the prevailing attitude to learning is not sufficiently urgent or competitive.

Leader in *The Times*, June 1974

7 Conservative Pragmatism

After a quarter of a century of left-wing possession of the educational initiative, an educational budget which is approaching the staggering figure of £4,000 million a year —well ahead of defence—and the continuous advance of the comprehensive school, we are left with unprecedented worry and alarm among parents about the quality of education which we are providing. In particular they are concerned over standards of conduct, discipline and learning, and horrified by the spread of truancy and violence. The trend of opinion is away from ideology towards pragmatism and in favour of taking a long, close look at what is actually happening in our schools as opposed to placing trust in the discredited prophets who can only tell us what should be happening.

Norman St John Stevas, *Daily Telegraph*, August 1974

8 Vandalism

Accidental damage and vandalism to Inner London school buildings has reached such high proportions that the I.L.E.A. has ordered a special inquiry into its 880 primary and 211 secondary schools to establish a league table of the high spenders.

. . . one I.L.E.A. comprehensive . . . spends £50 a day— £1,000 a month—on repairing broken glass alone.

T.E.S., January 1974

9 Declining Standards in Spelling

A substantial deterioration in the average level of spelling attainment since 1920 is one of the main findings of a research study carried out by a Staffordshire education psychologist, Mr David Cookson, and reported in the current *Journal of the Association of Education Psychologists*. Comparing the scores of 547 first- and third-year secondary school pupils on a standard test of spelling with the scores of similar age groups in 1920, spelling scores show a decline of between 12% for first years and 17.5% for third years.

T.E.S., January 1974

10 Industry's View of Modern Maths

Fierce opposition to modern maths is growing in industry, particularly among engineering firms, and among chemistry teachers in schools. Industrialists are finding they are having to teach their apprentices basic mathematical skills, such as decimals and percentages . . .

Mr Michael Bury, director of education at the Confederation of British Industry, said that their worry was a more general one about the falling standards in the three Rs. 'Very often we find ourselves doing what amounts to remedial work.'

T.E.S., February 1974

11 Truancy and ROSLA

Raising the school leaving age to 16 was a 'mindless error', Mr Harry Judge, director of Oxford University Department of Education told the Headmasters' Association conference in Oxford yesterday.

Experience in the United States had shown that keeping people in school when they did not want to be there would widen the gaps in achievement between pupils of different abilities, not narrow them.

Mr Judge, who was recently head of Banbury comprehensive school, once described by Mr Richard Crossman as one of the best schools in the country, told secondary school heads:

'The school leaving age should be lowered. The limits of compulsion have been passed.'

Sunday Telegraph, March 1974

12 Student Dialogue

On Friday, a group of students, who complain that Dr Sloman doesn't talk to them and call him the 'phantom Chancellor', pushed their way into his office for a spot of Essex-style dialogue and discussion.

Dr Sloman, who is 53, sat neatly in a grey suit and tie, smiled nervously and gave clipped answers. The students, with studied loutishness, put cigarettes out on the floor, swigged Coca-Cola from bottles and called him Albert.

'Albert, you're a bloody boring little academic,' said one student with a wispy Ho Chi Minh beard. A number of students called him a Fascist. One girl said, 'You silly old sod' and walked out of the room. The discussion was not considered fruitful by either side.

Dr Sloman has been facing irate students on and off now since Essex first began to have problems in 1968. Compared to now, these troubles were little ones, but they hit the headlines at the time.

Sunday Times, April 1974

13 What Next?

. . . Sir Keith Joseph, Shadow Home Secretary, suggested last night that a study of 'the very purposes and performance of our educational system' would surely be necessary one day.

'The present state of our system can give no joy to either Tory or Socialist or, more importantly, to any parent,' he said at Luton.

Daily Telegraph, October 1974